FINDING FREEDOM

Memorializing the Voices of Freedom Summer

Edited by Jacqueline Johnson *Jacqueline Johnson*
Foreword by Keith Beauchamp

Miami University Press
Oxford, Ohio

Copyright 2013, Miami University Press

Edited by Jacqueline Johnson
Cover design by Madge Duffey
Page design by Dana Leonard

Period photographs from the Freedom Summer training sessions held on the campus of Western College for Women are © George R. Hoxie, included courtesy of the Smith Library of Regional History, Oxford, Ohio; photographs of the memorial are © Dana Leonard.
"Freedom Ride" in *On the Bus with Rosa Parks* (W.W. Norton & Company, New York, NY) is © 1999 by Rita Dove. Reprinted here by permission of the author.

Library of Congress Cataloging-in-Publication Data

Finding freedom : memorializing the voices of freedom summer / edited by Jacqueline Johnson.
    pages cm
 ISBN 978-1-881163-52-7 (pbk.)
1. African Americans--Civil rights--Mississippi--History--20th century--Sources. 2. Civil rights movements--Mississippi--History--20th century--Sources. 3. Civil rights workers--Mississippi--History--20th century--Sources. 4. Civil rights workers--Ohio--History--20th century--Sources. 5. Freedom Summer Memorial (Oxford, Ohio) 6. Mississippi Freedom Project. 7. Voter registration--Mississippi--History--20th century--Sources. 8. Western College for Women--History--20th century. I. Johnson, Jacqueline, 1965-
 E185.93.M6F56 2013
 323.1196'0730762--dc23
                    2012045347

CONTENTS

A man looks at newspaper reports about the Freedom Summer training.

FOREWORD

> "No privileged group in history has ever given up anything without some kind of blood sacrifice, something." —Robert "Bob" Moses

The "Freedom Summer" of 1964 is known as a crucial moment in U.S. civil rights history, but it is one moment in a long and ongoing struggle. As we revisit what took place at Western College for Women, and the memorial that now honors those who took part in the struggle, we should not ignore the bravery of all those who challenged the "Jim Crow" system and showed themselves willing to sacrifice their lives in order to secure for African Americans the right to vote.

As a child growing up in Baton Rouge, I often heard the names of leaders such as Rev. George W. Lee of Belzoni, Mississippi, and Lamar "Ditney" Smith of Brookhaven, Mississippi. These men sacrificed their lives in order for us to have our votes counted at the polls. But it wasn't until as an investigative filmmaker I began looking into their cases that I truly understood the magnitude of what took place in the "bloody summer" of 1955. Rev. Lee was shot and killed while on his way home from speaking at an event held to register black voters. Lamar Smith was gunned down on the Lincoln County courthouse lawn in broad daylight for the same act. Two weeks after Smith's murder, Emmett Louis Till, a 14-year-old black Chicago youth, was murdered for whistling at a white woman in Money, Mississippi. All these murders took place during the 1955 election year. They were part of an effort to keep African Americans in their place, to intimidate them and prevent them from voting. Justice was never done in these cases; the men who committed the murders went free. This contributed to the hostile environment that Council of Federated Organizations members of the Freedom Summer Project entered into almost a decade later.

By the time 1964 rolled around, racial hostility in Mississippi was at an all-time high. As the Mississippi Summer Project began, the Ku Klux Klan, the Mississippi White Citizens' Council and other racist groups violently campaigned to preserve their way of life.

Tragedy would strike again. On June 21st, 1964, on their first day of Freedom Summer, James Chaney, a 21-year-old local black Mississippian; Andrew Goodman, a 20-year-old student at Queens College; and Michael Schwerner, a 24-year-old social worker and CORE Organizer from New York, drove to the African American community of

Longdale to investigate a recent church-burning orchestrated by the Klan. The three civil rights workers were arrested for allegedly speeding, detained and later released by the Neshoba County Deputy Sheriff, Cecil Price. They were never seen again.

On August 4, 1964, the FBI discovered the bodies of Chaney, Goodman, and Schwerner buried deep inside an earthen dam. Three years later, the U.S. Department of Justice charged 18 people with conspiring to deprive the activists of their civil rights by murder. Two of the main suspects charged were the Sheriff of Neshoba County, Lawrence Rainey, and the Deputy Sheriff who released the trio on that fateful night, Cecil Price. Eventually, Price and six others were found guilty while the rest of those charged evaded prosecution.

On June 21, 2005, 41 years to the day after the volunteers' disappearance, a Neshoba County jury convicted Edgar Ray "Preacher" Killen, a former Ku Klux Klan organizer and Southern Baptist minister, on three counts of manslaughter. Killen is currently serving 60 years for his role in the killings. Till this day, many believe that there are others who are still with us who should be brought to justice.

Although there's been much progress since the 1960s, the struggle for voters' rights continues to this day. Some states limit voter participation by limiting forms of acceptable identification, restricting where and when eligible voters may register and banning formerly incarcerated citizens from the polls. Many believe that this is a new form of "Jim Crow-ism."

When we consider the history of Freedom Summer and the role that COFO played in the Mississippi voters' movement and in solving other social ills that suppressed African Americans, we do well to remember the courageous actions of all those who contributed to the passage of the Civil Rights Act of 1964. Many of the volunteers who attended the two one-week training sessions in Oxford, Ohio were young, but they had the fortitude to set aside their own needs for a prophetic vision of change, a change that will forever benefit generations to come.

We all have a role to play and we must exercise our mission while we can to the best of our ability. We must continue to serve and protect one another. Life is a struggle. Let's resolve to do all that we can in this life to immortalize the spirit of Freedom Summer. That spirit is our key to solving the problems of the present and our passport to a prosperous future.

—Keith Beauchamp

LETTER FROM DEAN JUDITH SESSIONS

Tucked away in the Western College Memorial Archives in historic Peabody Hall on the Western Campus of Miami University is the Freedom Summer Collection, part of the record of a pivotal moment in our nation's history. Across from Peabody Hall on a wooded grassy hillside is an inspiring memorial to that moment, and to the training at this site of a group of courageous and committed volunteers who put their lives in harm's way to protect the voting rights of African Americans in the South.

Jacqueline Johnson, the Western College Archivist, has brought together a wonderful collection of memoirs and documents bringing that critical moment back to life. The memories of those involved in that struggle are illuminating and inspiring. I hope that students, teachers, historians and the general public will find this volume a worthy commemoration of their determination to fulfill the promise of freedom for all.

Miami University Libraries are honored to make the Freedom Summer Collection available to researchers interested in exploring this particular moment in the history of American civil rights.

—Judith A. Sessions
Dean & University Librarian
Miami University

Mississippi Freedom Summer Project 1964 Digital Collection
http://digital.lib.muohio.edu/fs/

FREEDOM SUMMER
AND
WESTERN COLLEGE FOR WOMEN

ANN ELIZABETH ARMSTRONG
THE MISSISSIPPI SUMMER PROJECT

The Mississippi Summer Project of 1964 was a complex and creative campaign that took place at a crucial turning point in the civil rights movement. It was part of a multipronged initiative designed to engage the entire nation with the plight of African Americans in Mississippi and shine the spotlight on the violence and injustice there. "Freedom Summer," as it would later be called,[1] involved a coalition of several organizations, but the Student Nonviolent Coordinating Committee (SNCC) was its driving force. In 1960, youth from sit-in movements founded the organization on a shared commitment to non-violent direct action and the empowerment of local communities. Throughout the early 1960s, SNCC developed direct action sit-in strategies, participated in Freedom Rides, started projects throughout the South, and eventually turned its focus to voting rights and voter education.[2] SNCC began their activism with sit-ins that tested new integration laws, but they generated an expansive vision of social change, as illustrated in the Summer Project of 1964.

From 1961 to 1963, SNCC initiated voter registration drives in Mississippi with little success. Frustrated by the escalating violence and the murders of key allies in the local Mississippi community, Bob Moses suggested that SNCC focus all its resources on Mississippi and reinvigorate its work by recruiting volunteers from a national pool of college students. In 1963, a similar small-scale effort called "The Freedom Vote" involving a few students from Yale and Stanford had generated significant media attention (Sinsheimer 217-244). But Moses' proposal was extremely controversial among those already committed to the movement. Why should uninformed outsiders be invited? They might jeopardize delicate relationships with local people, relationships forged through hard work. Would Mississippi blacks be able to work with privileged white college students as equals? Were nonviolent strategies still relevant and effective, particularly in the face of escalating violence from the white Mississippi community? Was integration still a goal or were there better ways to cultivate political power at the grassroots level? Did the activists have allies in the federal government or were these allies stalling on promises they had no intention of keeping?

---

1 Sally Belfrage named the campaign "Freedom Summer" in her 1965 book detailing the events she experienced as a volunteer. Until that time, the campaign was called "The Mississippi Summer Project" or just "Summer Project."

2 After the violent response to James Meredith's integration at University of Mississippi and Freedom Rides, the Kennedy administration urged SNCC to focus on voting rights instead of desegregation (Hogan 50).

Would bringing in these outsiders strain the capacity of SNCC's organization or, even worse, change it? Had they prepared the local Mississippi community enough for the influx of volunteer workers? (Clayborne 96-111; Hogan 143-154; McAdam 28-34)

These debates raged within SNCC as they planned their strategy and recruited volunteers for "the Summer Project" from all over the country. Voting rights were a key focus of SNCC's efforts in Mississippi. While the Mississippi population was 49% black, only 6.9% of that population was registered to vote (Andrews 69-70). Clearly very tangible social changes could take place if African Americans could vote. However, by this point in their efforts, activists knew just how enormous the obstacles to voting were, so Freedom Summer was much more than a voting rights campaign. There were three major focuses: 1) educating and registering African American voters; 2) teaching youth in Freedom Schools by providing instruction in core subjects while emphasizing black history and citizenship skills; and 3) building community centers that offered health care, recreation, and necessary social support systems. In addition to these three major focuses, there were other related efforts: public relations and communications, research projects, legal efforts, the Delta ministry project, the Medical Committee for Human Rights, the Free Southern Theater, and the "White Folk's Project," an effort to organize white working class allies in the Gulf Coast region. Freedom Summer was a comprehensive effort to reimagine Mississippi and introduce African Americans to the rights, privileges, and support systems enjoyed by other American citizens. Hence, SNCC needed to build communities from the ground up, addressing community needs while building a foundation for future grassroots activism.

In working towards these ambitious goals, Freedom Summer brought together three very different groups of people.[3] There were the civil rights movement activists from organizations like SNCC and Congress of Racial Equality (CORE). Most of these were northern-educated college students. There were local Mississippi citizens and activists. These risk takers were willing to endure reprisals, and many lost their jobs or family during their involvement with the movement (Dittmer 170-302). These Mississippi activists founded the Council of Federated Organizations (COFO), which managed the coalition of organizations running the summer project, and the Mississippi Freedom Democratic Party (MFDP), the political party that would challenge Mississippi's segregated Democratic party at the national convention. Finally, there were the volunteers, about 800 college

---

3   See Bruce Hartford's essay at http://www.crmvet.org/tim/fs64orgs.htm for more about the "Organizational Structure of the Mississippi Summer Project."

students who had been recruited from all over the country through universities, churches, and civil rights organizations.[4] In mid-June 1964, the three groups met in Oxford, Ohio at Western College for Women to prepare for the summer's work. The volunteers had applied for the summer project, providing references and undergoing interviews. Each volunteer provided funds for weekly housing and food expenses as well as bail in the event of arrest. Though Berea College in Kentucky was the initial site for the orientation, the National Council for Churches, the sponsor of the orientation, found Western College as a quick replacement when Berea pulled out in early May.[5]

The orientation that took place at Western College for Women in Oxford is significant for many reasons. It illustrates many of the growing pains social movements often experience as they reach out to recruit and train new members. Activists first had to train new volunteers in how to survive in Mississippi and then teach them how to register voters, teach in freedom schools, and organize community members. How could the activists transfer all of what had been learned in previous struggles to the new recruits? How could they cre-

ate a shared understanding of their goals and a unified sense of purpose? How could white students of privilege begin to understand the institutionalized oppression that the people of Mississippi had experienced? Because the Summer Project took place in 27 different counties (Holt 195) all over the state, the Oxford training was the one moment when all of the activists were in one place, making it an important opportunity to develop group solidarity and launch a publicity campaign. The national media eagerly filmed white college students preparing to nonviolently face violent opposition. SNCC activists had begun to wonder if the American public had become desensitized to images of black bodies facing violence. Would the American people become interested in the injustices in Mississippi if they saw their own sons and daughters in the front lines of the struggle?

The orientation piqued the interest of the public. And then, during the second week of training, Mickey Schwerner, James Chaney and Andrew Goodman went missing, and there was no doubt that this was a national story of historic proportions. The disappearance of the three men was exactly the situation that the training session had

---

4 In addition to these student volunteers, there were also 300–500 professionals, doctors, lawyers, clergymen and clergywomen, who volunteered for one to two weeks at a time throughout the summer (Hartford).

5 After a call from a Mississippi alum and trustee of Berea College, the president of Berea decided to withdraw in early May 1964 (Glowers). In addition to the training site of Western College, a small number of students who couldn't make it to Oxford in June were trained at LeMoyne College near Memphis (Adickes 50-51).

been preparing volunteers to avoid. From Oxford, SNCC appealed to the federal government for FBI help in finding the three men and federal protection for their volunteers for the rest of the summer (Cagin and Dray 1-46). By the end of the second week, activists knew that their friends who had just been with them in Oxford a few days before were dead. Bob Moses encouraged volunteers who had doubts to drop out of the project. Was the campaign taking irresponsible risks by sending volunteers to Mississippi? Or were they showing their solidarity with the Mississippi people who had endured such dangers for years?

The orientation took place over a two-week period with two different groups of volunteers. The first week focused on the voter registration drive and the second week focused on Freedom Schools and Community Centers.[6] In the mornings, students attended general sessions in lecture halls like Peabody's Leonard Theatre and Presser's Kelly Auditorium. Monday, Bob Moses and James Foreman introduced Mississippi conditions and gave an overview of the project. Tuesday, they focused on African American history and informed participants about white resistance in Mississippi.

Speakers including Reverend Vincent Harding and the lawyer Charles Morgan shared their experiences in the South with students. Wednesday's session explored nonviolence in a lecture by the Reverend James Lawson (the second week Bayard Rustin also lectured on nonviolence). Thursday's session covered legal issues and informed volunteers what to do if they were arrested and how to navigate the idiosyncrasies of the Mississippi justice system. Notable civil rights lawyers providing their expertise included Jess Brown, John Pratt and Jack Greenberg. Friday's session examined the role of the federal government, as John Doar from the Attorney General's office explained that there would be no federal protection. After learning about the state of affairs in Mississippi, volunteers were shocked and incredulous regarding the federal government's policies. Each afternoon, volunteers attended area meetings in classrooms to learn more about the specific community they would live in, or they learned project skills to apply to their work. Frequently, the afternoon sessions utilized role-playing workshops on the lawn to practice nonviolence or explore situations they might face within the black community ("Possible Role Playing Situations"). They needed to

6 For accounts of the first week of training consult Ellen Barnes' Journal in the Western College Memorial Archives, Tracy Sugarman's *Stranger at the Gates*, Len Holt's *The Summer That Didn't End*, Cleveland Sellars' *The River of No Return*, Stokely Carmichael's *Ready for Revolution*, and Elizabeth Sutherland-Martinez's *Letters from Mississippi*. For the second week, see Sally Belfrage's *Freedom Summer*, Jane Adams' Journal in the Western College Memorial Archives, and Elizabeth Sutherland-Martinez's *Letters from Mississippi*.

learn how to respond when arrested by a Southern policeman, and the volunteers also had much to learn about communicating with the local black community.

Many volunteers documented their daily experiences at the Oxford orientation in letters and journals. The various accounts reveal an atmosphere of tension and misapprehension during the first week of training, June 14-20. Many of the activists felt the volunteers were naïve, and they still doubted the premise of the summer project. Some volunteers complained that staffers were cliquish and aloof. When volunteers laughed at a racist voter registrar during the showing of a film about voting rights, the activists were so upset that they stormed out of the room, opening up a confrontation. Several documents describe a group therapy session in which staff had to explain their very real fears for the volunteers and volunteers had to confront cultural differences that had led to their insensitivity (Sutherland-Martinez 7-9; Sugarman 15-22). Schwerner, Chaney and Goodman were among those training the first week, and, by Sunday evening at the end of that week when the new batch of volunteers were arriving, staff thought that their worst fears about the three missing men might be confirmed. Monday of the second week of training, June 21-28, began with an interruption during the first overview session. Bob Moses and Rita Schwerner explained that Schwerner, Chaney, and Goodman had missed their check-in time the night before and the situation was dire. Immediately, volunteers were organized to write, telegram or call their congressmen to request federal assistance (Belfrage 8-12; Smith Young 245-246). While tensions among the volunteers and staff persisted during the second week, the disappearance of the three men set the tone, creating emotional bonding and a heightened sense of reality.

All orientation participants share one memory: the important role of singing freedom songs. Frequently Mississippi residents like Fannie Lou Hamer or some of the SNCC Freedom Singers led the songs. Sessions always began with singing and ended with singing. Several confrontations and awkward moments were disarmed with singing (Smith Young 246). And the media captured much of this singing, particularly in the angst-filled moments just before the second group left on the buses to go to Mississippi. While the moments of singing represented much of the intense group bonding taking place, volunteers also remember stark isolation, loneliness and soul searching as they began to contemplate their own mortality and the ethical dilemmas posed by civil rights.

The orientation for the Summer Project was too brief, especially considering the vast differences between the world of the volunteers, the SNCC activists, and Mississippi. Several volunteers relied on their nonviolence training as they endured arrests and harassment throughout the summer.[7]

Others found themselves in situations that summer where they had to improvise and do things they had little or no preparation to do. Still, the training that took place at Western College for Women was a critical threshold, one that activated important debates that would continue to develop within the civil rights movement and inspire a new cadre of activists who would go on to contribute to social change movements over the next decade (McAdam 199-233).

In Oxford, Ohio, few paid much attention to the presence of the orientation at Western College for Women during the first week of training. However, after the publicity about the disappearance of the three men, several debates ensued that would have a significant impact on the community. Despite the fact that they were not in the South, white supremacists in the area still managed to harass civil rights activists with threatening letters (Anonymous). Spies from the Mississippi Sovereignty Commission even attempted to infiltrate the training sessions. Occasionally staff and volunteers would encounter harassment at local restaurants and gas stations. After the second week

of training, Western College administrators took some heat from their alumnae who disapproved of the "rabble rousers." Community members debated the issues in the local paper, wondering if their community's "Oxford Ohio" byline attached to national news stories should be a point of pride or shame (White). Despite the fact that the administration of nearby Miami University had no knowledge of the activities across the street at Western, there were several Miami University faculty, students and staff who got involved with the orientation activities, and some even wound up volunteering for the summer.[8]

The most remarkable impact of the orientation sessions on the Oxford community happened through the formation of the Friends of the Mississippi Summer Project (FMSP). During the second week of training, several community members drifted over to the Western campus to witness the training sessions. The role-playing exercises in particular made a significant impact on them and galvanized them to take action. One young volunteer explained that she had been able to come for the summer because members of her church commu-

---

7 See Mississippi Summer Project Running Summary of incidents for an account of the constant stream of violence focused on the project (McAdam 257-268).

8 Two students from Miami University participated as volunteers: William Ninde (Hattiesburg Freedom School) and Margaret Dobbins (Columbus Freedom School). Ellen Barnes, another student, attended the orientation session. Roland Duerksen, who became a faculty member at Miami University, volunteered in Mississippi. Tom Tolg, a Miami graduate student, recruited volunteers for the Summer Project. One Western College for Women student, Judith Hampton, participated in 1965 in a project that continued past 1964.

nity had raised money for her subsistence funds. This group of concerned Oxford citizens swung into action (Stark; Delaney). They gathered books and supplies for the Freedom Schools, recruited sponsors for more than 30 volunteers to provide subsistence funds, helped fix cars so they couldn't be bombed, and raised money to support SNCC's transportation expenses down to Mississippi. Within the span of 48 hours, they had organized resources and a small community that would continue to meet as an organization and support the civil rights activists for the next two years ("Newsletter").[9] Their newsletters shared important news from the front lines and demonstrated their continued engagement with the activism in Mississippi and the national discourse on civil rights. While there were other "Freedom Centers" throughout the country that provided similar support to SNCC, the Oxford FMSP was among the strongest and best organized of such groups, proving that a small group of concerned citizens can make a difference. Miami University agreed to merge with Western College for Women in 1973 and, with this transition, community members have passed down the local history, but the dedication of the Mississippi Freedom Summer Memorial in 2000 was an important step in making a permanent marker of the site where events took place that transformed our nation.

In contrast to civil rights history that only tells us about leaders and martyrs, Freedom Summer adds new and important facets to our civil rights narratives. It illustrates the complexities of the grassroots organizing, the delicacies of coalition building, the unique power of youth-led activist movements, and the risk-taking and resistance that always come with social change. Freedom Summer activists found innovative and imaginative ways to speak truth to power and join Mississippi to the rest of the nation. At the same time, they placed the Mississippi people in charge of their own destiny, transforming political participation in local and national politics. Our world has changed dramatically since 1964, but there is still much to learn from these events as we study how a social movement opened up new possibilities to the nation.

Works Cited

Adams, Jane. Letter and Notes, Jane Adams' Notes from Freedom Summer Training, June 17-26, 1964. Mississippi Freedom Summer 1964 Digital Collection. Miami University. Web 2 Dec. 2011. http://digital.lib.muohio.edu/fs/item_viewer.php?CISOROOT=/fstxt&CISOPTR=1225&CISOBOX=1&REC=1.

Adickes, Sandra E. *The Legacy of a Freedom School.* New York: Palgrave Macmillan, 2005.

9 The Friends of the Mississippi Summer Project was primarily composed of white community members. There is also anecdotal evidence that members of the black community assisted activists by providing car repair and other services to activists.

Andrews, Kenneth T. *Freedom is a Constant Struggle: The Mississippi Civil Rights Movement and Its Legacy.* Chicago: University of Chicago Press, 2004.

Anonymous. Letter to John Lewis. 14 June 1964. The Student Nonviolent Coordinating Committee Records. Martin Luther King Library and Archives. Print.

Barnes, Ellen. Journal of Ellen Barnes' experiences at Western College during the Mississippi Freedom Project, 1964. Mississippi Freedom Summer of 1964 Digital Archive. Miami University. Web 2 Dec. 2011. http://digital.lib.muohio.edu/fs/item_viewer.php?CISOROOT=/fstxt&CISOPTR=1146&CISOBOX=1&REC=1.

Belfrage, Sally. *Freedom Summer.* Charlottesville: University of Virginia Press, 1965.

Clayborne, Carson. *In Struggle: SNCC and the Black Awakening of the 1960s.* Cambridge: Harvard UP, 1995.

Carmichael, Stokely. *Ready for Revolution.* NewYork: Scribner, 2003.

Cagin, Seth and Phillip Dray. *We Are Not Afraid: The Story of Goodman, Schwerner, and Chaney and the Civil Rights Campaign for Mississippi.* New York: Macmillian, 1988.

Delaney, Paul. "Mississippi Project: Oxford still talks of training meet." *The Dayton Daily News* (no date). Miami University. Mississippi Freedom Summer Project 1964 Digital Collection. Web 25 July 2012. http://digital.lib.muohio.edu/fs/item_viewer.php?CISOROOT=/fstxt&CISOPTR=877&CISOBOX=1&REC=3.

Dittmer, John. *Local People: The Struggle for Civil Rights in Mississippi.* Chicago: University of Illinois Press, 1995.

Gowler, Steven. Report, 'Berea College and the training of the civil rights workers', September 16, 2003. Mississippi Freedom Summer Project 1964 Digital Collection. Miami University. Web 2 Dec. 2011. http://digital.lib.muohio.edu/fs/item_viewer.php?CISOROOT=/fstxt&CISOPTR=1023&CISOBOX=1&REC=3.

Hartford, Bruce. "Organizational Structure of Freedom Summer, 1964." Civil Rights Movement Veterans Website. Bay Area Movement Veterans. Web 25 July 2012. http://www.crmvet.org/tim/fs64orgs.htm.

Hogan, Wesley. *Many Minds, One Heart: SNCC's Dream for a New America.* Chapel Hill: University of North Carolina, 2007.

Holt, Len. *The Summer That Didn't End: The Story of the Mississippi Civil Rights Project of 1964 and Its Challenge to the Future of America.* New York: William Morrow, 1965.

McAdam, Doug. *Freedom Summer.* New York and Oxford: Oxford UP, 1988.

Mississippi Sovereignty Commission On-line. http://mdah.state.ms.us/arrec/digital_archives/sovcom/.

"Newsletter of the Friends of the Mississippi Subsistence Project," 18 November 1964:5. Mississippi Freedom Summer Project 1964 Digital Collection, Miami University. Web 2 Dec. 2011. http://digital.lib.muohio.edu/fs/item_viewer.php?CISOROOT=/fstxt&CISOPTR=621&CISOBOX=1&REC=14.

"Possible role playing situations; undated." Zoya Zeman Collection. University of Southern Mississippi Digital Collections. Web 2 Dec. 2011. http://digilib.usm.edu/cdm/singleitem/collection/manu/id/184.

Sinsheimer, Joseph A. "The Freedom Vote of 1963: New Strategies of Racial Protest in Mississippi." *The Journal of Southern History*. Vol. 55, No. 2 (May, 1989): 217-244.

Smith Young, Jean. "Do whatever you are big enough to do." *Hands on the Freedom Plow: Personal Accounts by Women in SNCC*. Urbana: University of Illinois Press, 2010.

Stark, Mary. "Mississippi Project Friends Seek Donations to Aid Work." *The Oxford Press*. 2 July 1964. Mississippi Freedom Summer Project 1964 Digital Collection. Miami University. Web 25 July 2012. http://digital.lib.muohio.edu/fs/item_viewer.php?CISOROOT=/fstxt&CISOPTR=874&CISOBOX=1&REC=2.

Sugarman, Tracy. *Stranger at the Gates: A Summer in Mississippi*. New York: Hill and Wang, 1966.

Sutherland-Martinez, Elizabeth. Ed.. *Letters from Mississippi: Reports from Civil Rights Volunteers & Poetry of the 1964 Freedom Summer*. Brookline, MA: Zephyr Press, 2007.

White, Bob. "Why Blame Us?" *The Oxford Press*. 2 July 1964. Mississippi Freedom Summer Project 1964 Digital Collection. Miami University. Web 4 Dec. 2011. http://digital.lib.muohio.edu/fs/item_viewer.php?CISOROOT=/fstxt&CISOPTR=758&CISOBOX=1&REC=1.

RITA DOVE
FREEDOM RIDE

As if, after High Street
and the left turn onto Exchange,
the view would veer onto
someplace fresh: Curaçao,
or a mosque adrift on a milk-fed pond.
But there's just more cloud cover,
and germy air
condensing on the tinted glass,
and the little houses with
their fearful patches of yard
rushing into the flames.

Pull the cord a stop too soon,
and you'll find yourself walking
a gauntlet of stares.
Daydream, and you'll wake up
in the stale dark of a cinema,
Dallas playing its mistake over and over
until even that sad reel won't stay
stuck—there's still
Bobby and Malcolm and Memphis,
at every corner the same
scorched brick, darkened windows.

Make no mistake: There's fire
back where you came from, too.
Pick any stop: You can ride
into the afternoon singing with strangers,

or rush home to the scotch you've been pouring all day—
but where you sit is where you'll be
when the fire hits.

Bill Owsley of Miami's Architecture Department created the design for the Friends of the Mississippi Freedom Project (FMFP) cards, which were sold to raise money during the Christmas holiday season. The message read: "The hands of man reach out... / they grope in darkness and despair. / A light shines in the darkness... / And overcomes the darkness, / The light of HOPE / The light of DIGNITY / the light of FREEDOM."

Jane Strippel
FRIENDS OF THE MISSISSIPPI SUMMER PROJECT

Introduction

Shortly before noon, I heard the phone ring. I had been working out in the backyard of our home in Oxford, Ohio, all morning, weeding and planting perennials. Bob, my late husband, was calling from his office in Warfield Hall at Miami University where he served as the Assistant Dean of Men in the Division of Student Affairs. "I have some time this afternoon," he said. "Would you like to go over to Western with me to observe the student orientation?"

I was elated. He had shared the purpose and plans for the Mississippi Summer Project with me soon after President Herrick Young and the Western College Administrative staff had approved the request to host the training. This was the first week of the Project, which ran June 14–20, 1964.

I remember what a beautiful day it was; the flowering magnolias, dogwoods, and redbuds were still presenting their annual spring show around Oxford. As we walked up the hill toward old Peabody Hall, Bob explained that the general sessions were held there in Leonard Theater, usually in the morning, midafternoon, and evening. They offered an historical perspective on racism and covered topics such as stereotypes and myths about Negroes, black/white relations in Mississippi, the

theory and practice of nonviolence, legal issues, and confronting one's own prejudices. The workshops were mostly held outside on the Western campus grounds; students were sitting and lying down in groups large and small. We stopped to listen to the trainers and student interactions at some of them. One workshop I will never forget. It made such a deep impression on me. Volunteers were learning nonviolent self-defense techniques to prepare themselves for Mississippi. As they role-played various scenarios they might encounter, their bodies contorted to protect their heads and genitals, I realized what they were facing was more dangerous than I had previously thought. I felt an anxiety I had never experienced before.

Bob and I returned several times to observe the orientation sessions. Some of the students brought guitars, and there was frequent planned and spontaneous singing in between sessions and later in the evenings. We recognized many of the same songs sung by the famous Freedom Singers who appeared with Dick Gregory earlier that spring on April 29, 1964, at Miami's Withrow Court.

Formation and Activities of the Friends of the Mississippi Summer Project

"Friends of the Mississippi Summer Project," as it

was first called, was started by Oxford community members during the second week of the student volunteers' orientation at Western College for Women on June 28, 1964. One of the student volunteers had expressed to a few community members how much the support of her church and community back home had meant to her. They realized how important that kind of support would be if it were generated from the Oxford area. Approximately sixty local persons responded to the notice of a meeting held at Western College for Women to help provide moral and financial support to the volunteers.

Among the twenty-eight students were many who would normally work during the summer to meet their college expenses in the fall. Although SNCC had raised enough funds to enable them to return to college, the students needed what was termed "subsistence expenses" for living in and travel to and from Mississippi. They also needed typewriters, books and other supplies for their work in the Freedom Schools, community centers, and voter registration projects. A fund for bail money was also developed with pledges to provide money if any of the students were jailed.

The Friends planned to meet throughout the summer, and an executive committee was formed. We met for the first time on Sunday, June 28, 1964, from 3:00 to 7:00 p.m. at the home of Bill and Betsy Peabody. Members included Melvin Bloom,

Ann Fulton, Wendy and Bob Kisken, David T. Lewis, Art Miller, Reverend Bill Peabody, Mary Stark and myself. John Badgley, Assistant Professor of Government, Miami University, joined the committee in July and was responsible for contacting people in other universities for contributions to the FMSP Fund and for loans if bail was needed to release volunteers from jail. We elected Reverend Bill Peabody, Associate Rector, Holy Trinity Episcopal Church, as Chairman; Melvin Bloom, Professor of Mathematics at Miami University, as Treasurer; Robert Kisken as Assistant Treasurer; and Wendy Kisken, Instructor of French at Western College for Women, as Secretary.

A bank account was opened in Oxford under the name Friends of the Mississippi Summer Project or simply "FMSP." As of June 28, 1964, a total of $490 had been distributed to the volunteers for subsistence to last through July 4, 1964.

The first general meeting of "FMSP" was held on Monday, July 14, 1964, at 8:00 pm in the Holy Trinity Episcopal Church Undercroft. It included a report by three Oxford persons who had just returned from Mississippi, an exchange of letters from volunteers, and other news and announcements.

Newsletters were frequently sent out to FMSP members with announcements of upcoming meetings, quotes from volunteers' letters describing their experiences in Mississippi, activities of members, and updates on funds received. Wendy

Kisken was mainly responsible for the newsletter at first, and later the staff was expanded to include Dan Wozniak, editor; Irma Sandage, associate editor; Susan Bocher, news editor; and Dorothy Renfrow, letters.

Being a sponsor for one or more of the student volunteers was the most rewarding experience for FMSP members. Our family supported Barbara Simon, who worked in one of two Freedom Schools in Madison County, Mississippi. In one of her earlier letters dated July 14, 1964, she wrote that she and the other women were ordered to move out of the Freedom Houses because of the possible bad publicity. She and another volunteer who were now living with an elderly lady had a frightful experience one night when a man came asking to see them and stayed on the porch about fifteen minutes. He inquired if the lady had a shotgun, and when she told him it was none of his business he left.

She also noted that late model, radio-equipped cars of the Citizens Council passed by frequently, and one of the local COFO workers was told by a council member that the Freedom House would be bombed before the summer was over. They were taking special precautions.

Barbara felt her teaching was truly rewarding, and the kids attending the Freedom Schools were eager to learn the truths about the myths they had taken for granted and wished the Freedom Schools would be open all year.

Barbara received her mail in Canton, and warned us, since some of the students' mail was being opened, to send money by Postal Money Orders because Registered mail and checks were not safe.

The sponsors felt a very special, personal bond with their students. They became a part of our families. We felt greatly concerned when they left Oxford, particularly because of the disappearance of the three students James Chaney, Andrew Goodman, and Michael Schwerner, who left Oxford on June 20, 1964, after the first week of training and were later found murdered on August 4, 1964. We stayed glued to the daily national news reports.

Besides contributing money and needed supplies, sending letters to the student volunteers they were sponsoring, and encouraging others to attend meetings, the Friends helped in lots of other important ways. Don Nelson, Peter Anderson, and Art Miller neutralized the latches on the car hoods so they could only be opened from the inside to help protect the student volunteers. Don Nelson wrote Senator Ted Kennedy about a student, Cephas Hughes, who was hurt in a car accident while volunteering in Mississippi. The Senator wrote Cephas and thanked him for the important work he was doing there.

Bill and Barbara McKinstry often shared about their student, Gloria Wise, a Spelman College graduate, who had written to their children about her experience growing up in Mississippi and as a Freedom Summer volunteer.

When Paul and Lois Daniel had the money orders they sent to their student intercepted, they wrote Nicholas Katzenbach, the Acting Attorney General, about it.

Dave Lewis, from Miami's Department of Sociology, appeared on Channel 2 Dayton News on July 26, 1964, and spoke about the Mississippi Summer Project. Irma Sandage helped arrange pen pals for a volunteer working in Meridian, Mississippi.

Debbie Hawley helped pack six large boxes of books, toys and drawing materials in the basement of Peabody Hall from the Unitarian Fellowship of Hamilton to be sent to the COFO community centers in Columbus, Holly Springs and Meridian, Mississippi.

The Oxford Branch of the NAACP held a fundraising dinner for FMSP at Holy Trinity Episcopal Church and contributed $200.30 for their work. The bombing of a home and church in the McComb, Mississippi area on September 21, 1964, followed the departure of most of the summer volunteers and a decrease in FBI staff when the summer project was over.

SNCC staff and local residents feared that harassment, intimidation and violence would increase and decided that the Mississippi Project needed to continue. The success of the Freedom Schools and voter registration efforts also informed their decision. The name "Friends of the Mississippi Summer Project" was changed to "Friends of the Mississippi Subsistence Project." The Friends enthusiastically agreed to continue supporting the remaining student volunteers along with new volunteers who needed financial help.

At the general meeting of FMSP on November 23, 1964, new officers were elected unanimously and took over their duties on January 1, 1965. Elected Chairman was Reverend Leonard Confar of the Oxford United Methodist Church. The Vice-Chairman was Anne Fulton, an instructor in Biology, Western College. The Recording Secretary was Mary White, a community member. The corresponding secretary was Wendy Kisken. The Treasurer was Clark Crannel, Professor of Psychology, Miami University, and the Publicity Chairman was Christine Van Gordon, Assistant Director of Bureau of Recommendations, School of Education, Miami University. Also at the meeting the group voted to change its name from Friends of the Mississippi Subsistence Project to Friends of the Mississippi Freedom Project. Bill Owsley of Miami's Architecture Department created the design for the Friends of the Mississippi Freedom Project (FMFP) cards, which were sold to raise money during the Christmas holiday season. The message read: "The hands of man reach out... / they grope in darkness and despair. / A light shines in the darkness... / And overcomes the darkness, / The light of HOPE / The light of DIGNITY / the light of FREEDOM."

Letters from Mississippi

In each issue of the FMSP Newsletter we looked forward to reading the "Mississippi Report" with letters received from the volunteers to their sponsors. These letters helped us learn what was happening all over Mississippi during Freedom Summer. A few examples from the newsletters:

July 14, 1964, Newsletter: Ruleville, Mississippi. "The home industry plan developed in response to the firing of many plantation workers who had become involved in registration work. A group of Ruleville women started a quilt making industry. Another group of women used waste stuffing to make hats. The home industries provided an economic base in the Negro community which would not be susceptible to pressure from the White Citizens' Councils."

August 5, 1964, Newsletter: "Generally, enrollments in Freedom Schools are higher than expected and student enthusiasm runs high. In rural Madison, Freedom Schools had expected only eighty students. Now, more than three hundred are enrolled in three schools. In Greenwood, sixty-seven senior high school students registered in the Freedom School. "In spite of threats of personal violence and actual loss of jobs, many local citizens continue to courageously support the summer project."

November 18, 1964, Newsletter: "The adults of McComb County live in constant fear that they may lose life, limb or property. This year alone in the McComb area there have been recorded five murders, twenty-seven bombings, fifty beatings and no arrests…we've had six bombings in the last three days. The room in which I'm writing this is still lacking the wall which was blasted away last July."

November 18, 1964, Newsletter: "We slept on the floor at night to avoid gunshots which might come through the windows."

November 18, 1964, Newsletter: "I really appreciate your concern and meeting you and the other warm and wonderful people in Oxford strengthened my belief in the basic goodness of man."

Oxford Community Response

Our small college community in southwestern Ohio was not unlike many communities in 1964 regarding attitudes toward racial matters. Beginning in 1950, segregation attitudes and policies began to change in Oxford, but they evolved slowly. Oxford restaurants became integrated, and the Oxford city pool was integrated in May 1950 after the local chapter of the NAACP took the town to the Butler County Court of Common Pleas. In 1954 the Oxford Movie Theater chose not to enforce the segregation era policy of seating Negroes in the back on the left side.

In the fall of 1968, four years after Freedom Summer, McGuffey Lab School revised its admission policy to allow non-white children to attend. There were few blacks hired by the city and the schools then.

In the spring of 1964 during the visit of Dick Gregory and the Freedom Singers, an angry group gathered outside Withrow Court on the Miami University campus shouting protests against their appearance. A brick was thrown through a window during the program.

When President Herrick Young of Western College for Women agreed to host the summer training after several colleges had refused, he was criticized by some in Oxford who felt the training was too controversial.

There were those who felt the students were just going to Mississippi for "a good time" or to "cause trouble," echoing many Southerners who believed these northern students had no business meddling in their affairs. An *Oxford Press* editorial also expressed this negative view. One of the "Friends" of the Mississippi Summer Project reported that his boss threatened that he might lose his job by associating with those "beatniks" and "trouble makers!"

On the other hand, many Oxford citizens supported the "Project" and believed we had a moral obligation to be involved. Letters of support were printed in the *Oxford Press*, including one by Western College's Dean of Students Phyllis Hoyt, who clearly communicated the purpose and the historical significance of the "project." Camilla Flinterman included in her letter of support the letter her family's sponsored student volunteer had written to her two daughters, Wendy and Carroll, about conditions in Mississippi that especially impacted children.

United Church Women of Oxford made an area-wide appeal for contributions to help support Mrs. Chaney following the murder of her son, James, after the first week of training. Over $537 was raised, and postal money orders were sent to her regularly by Jane Savage, a Presbyterian campus minister, as well as myself, to help pay her rent, utilities, and other expenses, since she had lost her job at a bakery.

One citizen wrote a letter to the Chairman of the "Friends" executive committee suggesting we "invite Mrs. Chaney to come to Oxford to make her home here, [welcoming] her children [to] attend our schools [while] we help find employment for her… [and] offer her our friendship and perhaps some assurance that there is still good in humanity."

Although there were these mixed feelings among Oxford citizens at the time of the Freedom Summer training, the spirit of those who wholeheartedly gave their support has made a difference through the years to this present day as more people realize the historical significance of the project.

The United Church Women's national program on "Assignment: Race," which took place in Oxford and many other communities around the country, began in 1961. Interracial discussion groups in the homes of participants helped to develop friendships and the greater understanding that has lasted all these years in Oxford. Another important outcome was a joint effort with the League of Women Voters of Oxford in a door-to-door campaign to promote integrated housing. Caroline Lindsay, one of the participants who later moved with her family to Chapel Hill, North Carolina, said, "I think these early gatherings and sharings helped to create a climate that made it somewhat easier for the Friends of the Mississippi Project to find support in Oxford in 1964."

Caroline's husband, Rev. Dr. Paul Lindsay, and his colleague Jane Savage, both Presbyterian campus ministers in Oxford, participated in another civil rights program with other Presbyterian ministers from the North to boycott Birmingham's largest department stores which refused to hire Negroes, desegregate lunch counters, restrooms, and water fountains. It was organized by the Alabama Christian Movement for Human Rights.

Rev. William Peabody, Chairman of the Friends of the Mississippi Project, had the opportunity to speak to the faculty orientation of the Proctor Academy in Vermont as a member of their board in 2004 about his experience with the "Friends" in 1964. Focusing on the responsibility of the individual in a democratic community, he said, "There is a certain intersect of tension set up when we choose to live in any community and especially a Democratic one. The intersect is a pull between 'me as me' and 'me as a part of.' To be 'faithful' to the experiment one is called to remain within this tension for that is where life is found. The other choices are to 'spin off' out of the tension becoming uninvolved and isolated or to 'sell out' to the pressure of the community and become 'swallowed up.' The ever-present challenge is to stick with the ongoing dialogue between self and community, which in turn gives birth to the values of the community. I knew back then in Oxford that if I lived within this intersect of self and community, something could be born, a new energy and direction: The Friends of the Mississippi Summer Project."

The Significance of the Freedom Memorial

The idea for a Freedom Memorial on the Western College campus grew from seeds planted by several persons close to the Mississippi Freedom Project. They were Jane Goldflies, assistant to Dean Curt Ellison, Western College; Arthur Miller, President of the Oxford Branch NAACP; and Dr. William Stitt of Oxford Internal Medicine. Each in their own way helped to provide the vision and energy needed to make it finally happen when Miami University took the initiative in 2000.

I believe the Freedom Memorial on Miami University's Western campus is a beautiful and meaningful testament to what James Chaney, Michael Schwerner, and Andrew Goodman stood for. Andrew Goodman had told his mother, Carolyn, when she hugged him just before he left for the Mississippi Summer Project, "Mom, look, this is something I believe in and you believe in. All your life, you and Dad have said that this is not right — the Constitution is being violated."

The Freedom Memorial is a testament to all those courageous black citizens of Mississippi and throughout the South who risked their lives every day to welcome and support the student volunteers and other civil rights workers trying to help them win their freedoms. They had silently suffered the daily injustices, beatings, and lynchings long before 1964. Many died without ever being found, and their cases were never prosecuted.

But the Freedom Memorial serves not only as a testament to those martyrs. It stands as a reminder to each of us of our responsibility today and throughout our lives to work diligently in our own communities to address racism anywhere it raises its ugly head. We all need to have the courage to do what they did. As Frances Moore Lappé, a writer and activist for social change, has said, "Refuse to be bystanders or victims of history."

The Friends group of sponsors, their student volunteers and Mississippi locations included:

Mr. & Mrs. Peter Anderson
    Karl Morgan, Meridian

Mr. & Mrs. John Badgley
    John Buffington, Columbus

Mr. & Mrs. Joseph Backor
    Daniel Wood, Canton

Mrs. Lettie Bergstrom
    Fred Miller, Ruleville

Mr. & Mrs. T.A. Bisson
    Daniel Wood, Canton

Mr. & Mrs. Melvin Bloom
    Dorie Latner, Jackson

Mr. & Mrs. Joseph Cantrell
    Wendy Weiner and Paul Klein, Greenwood

Mr. & Mrs. Reo Christenson
    Sheilagh O'Brien, Moss Point

Mr. & Mrs. R.J. DeMar
Gloria Wise, Greenwood

Mr. & Mrs. Paul Daniel
Judy Walborn, Greenwood

Mr. & Mrs. James H. Davis
E.J. Brisker, Greenwood

Mr. & Mrs. Roland Delattre
Karen Duncan, Greenwood

Mr. & Mrs. Thomas Evans
Wayne Yancey, Holly Spring

Mr. & Mrs. Peter Flinterman & Cornell Hewson
Jennie Franklin, Carthage

Mr. & Mrs. R.B. Fulton
Barbara Walker, Holly Spring

Mr. & Mrs. N. Gottfried
E.J. Brisker, Greenwood

Mr. & Mrs. David Griffing
Harriet Tansman, Holly Spring

Rev. & Mrs. W.N. Hawley
Sherry Everett, Jackson

Mr. & Mrs. Eldon Hill
Gwen Robinson, Laurel

Mrs. Betty Howard
Sherry Everett, Jackson

Mr. & Mrs. Carl Jantzen
Linnell Barrett, Laurel

Mr. & Mrs. Robert Kisken
Georgia Martin, Pascagla

Mr. & Mrs. David T. Lewis
Margaret Dobbins & Brenda Travis, Columbus

Mr. & Mrs. Stanford Luce
Allen Goodner, Clarksdale

Mr. & Mrs. Philip Morsberger
Wayne Yancey, Holly Spring

Mr. & Mrs. William McKinstry
Gloria Wise, Greenwood

Mr. & Mrs. Arthur Miller
Allen Goodner, Clarksdale

Mr. & Mrs. Donald Nelson
Cephas Hughes, Holmes County

Mr. & Mrs. Robert Newman
Greg Kaslo, Hattiesburg

Rev. & Mrs. William Peabody
Wendy Wiener and Paul Klein, Greenwood

Mrs. Eleanor Price
Edith Black, Holmes County

Mr. & Mrs. C.J. Raeth
E.J. Brisker, Greenwood

Mr. & Mrs. Louis Renfrow
Lorne Cress, Hattiesburg

Mr. & Mrs. Orton Stark
Edith Black, Holmes County

Mr. & Mrs. Ralph Stone
 Ely Zaretsky, Greenwood

Mr. & Mrs. Robert Strippel
 Barbara Simon, Madison

Mr. John Weigel
 Dorothy Louie, Holly Spring

Mr. & Mrs. Archie White
 Jennie Franklin, Carthage

Mr. Milton White
 Mario Savio and Marshall Ganz, Holmes
 County

Mr. & Mrs. Walter Zimmer
 John Buffington, Columbus

To heal the brokenhearted,
to preach deliverance to the captives, . . .
to set at liberty them that are bruised.

(Mrs. Chaney and son Ben at
Memorial service for James
Chaney.)

On June 21, 1964 three civil rights workers
were murdered in Philadelphia, Mississippi. One
of these was James Chaney the 21 year old son of
Mrs. Fannie Lee Chaney of Meridian, Mississippi.

Mrs. Chaney has not only had to bear the loss
of a son, but has constantly been subjected to harassment and bomb threats. She has lost her job in
a local bakery and has been unable to find employment in Meridian. John Griffin, author of "Black
Like Me" and recent lecturer at Miami University
and Western College stated that Mrs. Chaney is in
urgent need of financial support for herself and
her 3 small children. At this time she has no
means of meeting her basic living expenses, which
include rent, gas, electricity, and also such items
as school lunches and bus fare for her children.

LET US DEMONSTRATE THROUGH OUR GIVING TODAY
OUR BELIEF IN THE PROMISE OF HOPE FOR ALL MEN
WHICH THIS CHRISTMAS SEASON PROCLAIMS.

(Appeal sponsored by United Church Women of Oxford)

United Church Women of Oxford made an area-wide appeal for contributions to help support Mrs. Chaney following the murder of her son. Over $537 was raised, and postal money orders were sent to her regularly by Oxford residents.

Volunteers gathered on lawn on Western campus in front of Clawson Hall singing freedom songs.

CHUDE ALLEN
MY PARENTS SAID YES!

I was twenty years old, a junior in college, when I wrote my parents that I wanted to apply to be a Freedom School teacher in the Mississippi Summer Project.[1] Since I was a girl and not yet twenty-one, I needed their permission. It was against the law for blacks and whites to live and work together in Mississippi, and they knew I might be put in jail or beaten, perhaps killed. Even though my parents had never been to a demonstration or walked on a picket line, I was sure they would say yes.

They'd let me come to Spelman College as an exchange student that spring. Spelman is a black women's college in Atlanta, Georgia. In 1964 I was one of thirteen white students among 706 African American students. All spring I'd been writing letters home telling them about what I was learning about racism and segregation in my classes, about my discussions with other students and the conferences and mass meetings I attended. I wrote about the philosophy of pacifism and nonviolent direct action. I told them about my experiences on picket lines at segregated restaurants in downtown Atlanta. And I described the plans for the Mississippi Summer Project, even before I decided I wanted to apply.

I also wrote them about my new best friend. She lived in Montgomery, Alabama. I couldn't visit her home during spring vacation because I was white and she was black. She told me it would be too dangerous for us to be together. "I am no longer an outsider," I wrote my parents. "This system has hurt me."

Not everyone who went to Mississippi that summer or who participated in the civil rights movement would say they had been willing to die. Most would probably say—as some of my friends have said—that they were willing to risk dying, but didn't really believe it would happen. I did think I might die. I wrote my parents that they might have to sacrifice a daughter.

I was a devout Christian and believed God wanted me to go to Mississippi. I was willing to die for the right of whites and blacks to live together and be treated equally. As a Christian, I believed in the concept of redemptive suffering, sacrificing oneself for something greater. Jesus, after all, had died for our sins. I wanted to help redeem the United States from the terrible sin of racism.

That was the philosophical belief underlying my willingness to risk my life teaching in a Freedom School

[1] That's what we called it. The term "freedom summer" was created by one of the summer volunteers, Sally Belfrage. It was the title for her book about her experience at the training at Western College for Women and then in Greenwood, Mississippi.

in Mississippi. Not being able to visit my friend in Montgomery, Alabama was the personal reason.

I think the fact that I wrote to my parents all spring, sharing with them what I was learning, helped them make the decision to allow me to go to Mississippi. It was especially difficult for my father, who was a manager in a rubber goods factory. The other managers did not support the civil rights movement. My mother, who was a nursery school teacher in our small community, didn't face the same opposition. Yet, as I've said, they weren't activists, and they knew I might die.

What, then, enabled them to sign that permission slip? They too were devout Christians and could not refuse me when I said I believed God wanted me to be part of this attempt to break the racist stranglehold in Mississippi. Yet it wasn't just signing that permission slip. They were tested again and again.

We lived in eastern Pennsylvania. I arranged to ride with a couple of volunteers who were driving from New York City to Western College for Women in Ohio for our week-long training before we went to Mississippi. My parents drove me to an exit on the Northeast Extension of the Pennsylvania Turnpike where we were to meet the volunteers.

There was no restaurant or public phone at the turnpike exit (and no cell phones in 1964). My father parked by the side of the road and we waited. The evening grew dark, but no car came. I sat in the back seat, my parents in the front. We knew we might never see each other again. We sat there all night. Dawn had come before the Volkswagen bug pulled up. The car had broken down, but there had been no way to tell us. I climbed into the car and we started for Ohio. Years later Mother would tell me that that night was one of the hardest of her life.

We were in the second group of trainees, Freedom School teachers, and community center volunteers. On the first day of our training we learned that three of the voter registration workers were missing. Rita Schwerner, wife of one of the missing men, stood on the stage of the auditorium and told us to organize by our home states, pool our money and call home. We were to mobilize our parents to call and write their congressmen, the Justice Department, and the president, demanding that the federal government find the three who were missing and protect all civil rights activists.

Twenty-five years later in the fall of 1989 I sat on the floor of my mother's living room and read through the papers she'd saved in the bottom drawer of her desk. I learned from a carbon copy of one of my father's letters to my grandfather that a congressman Dad had written had called him at work and told him to "get her the hell out of there." Dad wrote that he'd told the congressman the question wasn't getting me out, but guaranteeing the safety of all civil rights workers. He never told me.

The last night before we left for Mississippi, Bob

Moses, the director of the Mississippi Summer Project, looked at his feet as he talked about how difficult it was for him to send us in, knowing three were already dead even though their bodies had not been found, sending us in not knowing how many of us would die. Speaking softly, his eyes on his shoes, he told us, "All I can say is that I'll be there too."

The group sang as one. The words "They say that freedom is a constant struggle" burned in my heart. I knew we carried with us the spirits of James Chaney, Andrew Goodman, Mickey Schwerner, and all the people who had died and would die for freedom. We sang their souls into the sinews of our bodies. It did not matter whether I lived or died. I believed the movement would flourish and love would triumph over hate.

Yet I didn't appreciate my parents' courage. They could have stopped me from going into Mississippi as some girls' parents did. They could have made me come home. Instead they told me they loved me. They joined with other parents in the Philadelphia, Pennsylvania area for mutual support and to raise money for the freedom movement. They duplicated my letters and sent them to relatives, friends, supporters, and the press. By the end of the summer they were distributing 80 copies.

It was not an easy summer for them. They looked forward to my coming home. Yet when I did come home, I couldn't adjust. I was distant and uncommunicative. It was especially difficult for my mother. She became so distraught she wrote a letter to Carolyn Goodman, the mother of Andrew Goodman, who'd been murdered that summer. "You lost a son," she wrote, "but I lost a daughter."

Of course she knew it wasn't the same. She didn't send the letter; I have it among my things. But her suffering was real. It took a full year before I could share my feelings with her.

In 1989, the same year that I found my father's letter about the congressman telling him to get me out of Mississippi, I spoke at an assembly at my old high school. Mother came with me. I told the students I'd had to have my parents' permission to go. I said, "My mother is here today; even though she was scared, she let me go." Mother stood up. The students and faculty began clapping. She was a small woman, surrounded by people honoring her. Unfortunately, my father had already passed away. How I wish he too could have felt the faculty and students' appreciation for what he'd done.

My parents and I had the chance to contribute to making the world a better place. Regardless of the consequences, they joined me in the struggle to bring justice and equality to this country. That week when I was at Oxford was a time of soul-searching for both my parents and myself. They could have called me home. Like me they had come to understand that none of us can be free until all of us are free.

Freedom Summer volunteers in a training session at Western College with SNCC staff, learning about nonviolent resistance training. Carole Colca is featured in foreground.

Carole Colca
REFLECTIONS ON A LIFE-CHANGING EXPERIENCE

The 1964 Mississippi Summer Project, or what has become better known as Mississippi Freedom Summer, was 49 years ago. Yet to me it sometimes seems like just yesterday! Although I was directly involved for only four months, it stands out as one of the defining periods in my life. It certainly defined who I was at 21 years of age, and it still partially defines who I am today at 70 years of age. Reflecting on my experience can still put a lump in my throat and tears in my eyes. So many scenes, people, feelings, and impressions are crystal clear in my memory. Other memories are now fuzzy, and many details or experiences I read about by others who were there seem to have been deleted from my mind. I greatly regret not keeping a journal. What I record in this essay is based on my current recollections and perceptions. The challenge is to condense the depth and breadth of that life-changing experience into a short essay.

I have often been asked: "Why did you go?" The answer is not complicated. It was perfect timing. A couple months before I was to graduate from the University of Iowa, a representative of SNCC came to the campus to speak about the civil rights activities in Mississippi and, in particular, to recruit volunteers for the Mississippi Summer Project. I was a sociology major, passionate about so-cial justice and particularly racial equality. I had gone to the March on Washington the previous summer and participated in a few protests on campus, but, by and large, I was more idealistic than knowledgeable about the civil rights movement. I had just broken off an engagement to be married that summer, had no job lined up, felt free to do whatever, and the prospect to volunteer for civil rights work in Mississippi just felt right. I was the first to line up for an application. Two months later I was on my way to Western College for Women in Oxford, Ohio, for the orientation, much to my parents' consternation.

The week of intense preparation and training in Oxford was mind-blowing for me. I had no idea when I signed up just how dangerous this work might be. I had read and heard about the black people in the South being beaten and arrested and even lynched when protesting or defying the Jim Crow barriers. But surely nobody would dare hurt white student volunteers from the North. After all, wasn't it a primary premise of the summer project that the volunteers would be bringing the eyes and ears of their white middle-class friends and families, and with them, national publicity and pressure for federal protection? But the orientation leaders, all veterans of the civil rights movement and mostly native black Mississippians, quickly burst my illusions of security. The role-playing, the nonviolent self-defense they taught us, the many personal stories they recounted and movies we watched brought reality to life for us. The more I understood, the more appalled I was with the degree of oppression, intimidation, and violence against blacks accepted by white society as the "Southern way of life." The more inspired I was by the SNCC and CORE staff, the more committed I became. I don't recall having any reservations. More disturbing to me was the self-reflection they demanded from us. What was our real motivation? Did we have fantasies of heroism? Was it just a form of rebellion against parents? Were we just looking for an adventure? Did we secretly harbor fantasies of taboo romantic or sexual experiences? I lay awake at night questioning myself. I remember being impressed with the other volunteers I met, who seemed more experienced and knowledgeable and had more to offer than I did. I had never had a problem of low self-esteem, but I felt out of my element. So my doubts were all about my worthiness, not my willingness.

The most vivid memory I have from the orientation was the day Robert Moses gathered everyone together in the auditorium and told us of the three missing civil rights workers who had just gone to Mississippi the previous week, after the first orientation. One of them, Andrew Goodman, was a newly recruited white student volunteer, very much like me. Moses, visibly shaken, made the stunning statement that it was very likely they had been murdered. With much emotion he told us that he felt he was leading a group of sheep to their slaughter and urged each of us to call our families and think through whether we wanted to continue, assuring us that no one would think less of us if we decided to leave. As I think back on that time, I can only recall how much I respected Moses for his genuine concern for us. I don't recall having any dilemma whatsoever over whether or not to stay. In reviewing the couple of letters I wrote home during that week, I am puzzled why I never even mentioned this event. However, to paraphrase myself in one letter, I did say: "It is going to be more dangerous than I thought, but the Negroes in Mississippi live with the risk of being beaten or killed all the time, and my life is no more valuable than theirs."

Another very clear memory I have was the emotional impact of the Freedom Singers. They were the catalysts bonding us together. Joining hands and singing freedom songs with them, along with the COFO staff and the other volunteers, black and white together, sharing common values and purpose, infused me with this grand feeling of being part of a force so much greater than myself. It was a profoundly moving experience. Singing freedom songs continued to have that effect throughout the summer, whether it was with a handful of us or at a community gathering or COFO meetings.

Along with ten or eleven other volunteers, I was assigned to "Harmony Community," a small and unique all-black rural hamlet in central Mississippi, near the city of Carthage. Almost all of the several hundred families residing there owned their modest homes on land bought by their fathers and grandfathers after being freed from slavery. Some, besides farming their land, also worked in factories or as domestics in Carthage, but for the most part they were a unique community of people who felt less dependent on and beholden to the "white folks" for their sustenance, unlike most Mississippi Negroes. There was already a core of local people who were active in NAACP activities, fighting for the right to register to vote and protesting Jim Crow barriers. They had even filed and won a school desegregation lawsuit, which they hoped to test in the fall, starting with the first grade. I was designated to be a "community center worker," which meant working with the kids younger than Freedom School age, providing adult literacy classes (for which I was trained during orientation), developing a library, and whatever else the community wanted.

After a rather clandestine car trip to Mississippi, we finally arrived in the Harmony Community, and pulled up to a rundown abandoned schoolhouse with a multitude of people out in the yard waiting to welcome us. What a great memory I have of that moment! There was excitement among the volunteers as well as the local people.

It was immediately obvious who the local community leaders were. Winson and Cleo Hudson, and Winson's sister, Dovie, were confident and outspoken. They enthusiastically told us the plans for us to fix up the schoolhouse to use for the Freedom School and community center. Many were uncomfortable looking us in the eye or calling us by our first names without a "Miss" or "Mister," though they were as old as our parents and grandparents. They had never related to white people as equals or colleagues. But they were all welcoming and optimistic. After initial greetings, we gathered in a circle, joined hands, and sang a few freedom songs. I have never felt so sure that I was in the right place at the right time. They advised us to go into Carthage and introduce ourselves to the "officials" at the courthouse to let them know we were there and hopefully temper their hostility in anticipating "outside agitators." It was to be my first encounter with the mindset we had been prepared for. During our meeting, we remained polite and respectful but steadfast, as we were trained to do, while they laughed at us and condescendingly told us how foolish we were and how little we understood *their* niggers, who we would soon find were lazy, ignorant, etc. I particularly remember one saying, "Do you people understand that there are nothing but niggers living in that community?"

The next day an even larger number of men, women, and children turned up early in the morning, ready to get to work cleaning out and fixing up the school building. We worked in the blazing heat all morning. A group of the "officials," including the county school superintendent, pulled up and stood watching us for an hour or so, laughing and snickering, until finally they called us over to say that the building was county property and we had no right to use it and needed to vacate the property. This was disputed to no avail. (The school had been built by their fathers and grandfathers, funded by the Rosenthal Foundation.) The "officials" left smugly, leaving the local people frustrated but undaunted. They talked it over, then gathered everyone together and told us that if the COFO legal experts could not win the building back for us to use, we would have the Freedom School classes under the trees and use the one church in Harmony as a community center. Meanwhile we would find a way to build our own community center/ freedom school! That's exactly what we did the rest of the summer. For me this was an example of what the black people of Mississippi had been up against for years, for generations, and an example of how they endured. If you can't go through, go around; if you can't go around, go under; if not under, then over. But you keep on going.

My host family was led by Dovie Hudson, one of the indomitable community leaders. She was a widow with four of her eleven children still living at home (daughters ages 13–18), and a nine-year-old granddaughter. Two grown sons who lived locally also stayed at the house off and on. She was the soft-spoken and less articulate sister, but as determined and fearless as anyone I've ever met. It was a risk, of course, to house any of the civil rights volunteers. The night before we arrived a group of hoodlums drove through the community and shot into her house. It surprises me, looking back, how easily I seemed to adapt to the lifestyle, which was quite a change from the urban middle class conveniences I was accustomed to. There was electricity but no indoor plumbing, not even an outhouse. We washed up under a rigged-up shower a ways behind the house. As my co-volunteer, Jane Adams, also staying with Dovie Hudson, says in her journal, "We bathed naked to the stars and the pigs and the trees." The house was comfortable but very small for the eight of us. The nearest neighbor was her sister, a quarter mile down the road. There was a TV, but only one or two channels and few programs. I remember spending most evenings shelling peas and talking, sharing stories, often with visiting neighbors, or listening to the radio, doing the girls' hair or preparing for the next day's activities. There were no telephones in the community. Telephone wires and paved roads ended as you entered the one road into Harmony. There was one small grocery store, with a gas pump, in the center of the community. This was the gathering place for chatting, playing cards and checkers, or greeting each other coming and going. We walked the red dirt roads everywhere, in the unrelenting heat, unless we could hitch a ride in the back of a pickup truck. Meals were very basic. Yet I don't recall ever yearning for the conveniences I left behind. While sharing everyday life with the Hudsons, I became very fond of them, and I found it hard to leave when the time came to say goodbye.

The role of the community center worker was very unstructured and flexible. I spent most of my days organizing activities for the elementary school age children during Freedom School hours and the teenagers after their classes. Sometimes we did arts and crafts, sometimes produced plays from books or fairy tales we would modify to relate to their lives, and sometimes studied black history. We discussed and debated civil rights issues. We shared stories about ourselves and the differences in our life experiences. Whatever the activity, the objective was to broaden horizons, confront the false notion of the inferiority of Negroes, and raise their hopes, aspirations, and self-esteem. Several hours a week I had the rewarding experience of teaching two of the men in the community how to read. I also spent much of my time helping build the community center, which became a summer-long community project. Toward the end of the summer, we became busy canvassing the community to encourage parents of first graders to register their children at the white school, to enforce the desegregation suit that Ms. Hudson had won through the support of the NAACP.

Of course, I cannot write of my experiences that summer without telling at least one of the "war stories" that exemplify the hostility and violence we experienced from the local "white folks" and particularly from organizations like the Ku Klux Klan, the White Citizens Council, and Americans for the Preservation of the White Race (APWR). That hostility created the need for our constant watchfulness and the tension that permeated our everyday life. In order to make occasional phone calls home, or to our hometown newspapers, we had to go to the public phone booth in the middle of the town square in Carthage. We only went around dusk, after all the stores were closed and the streets were nearly empty. On one such occasion, I was stopped by the police as I crossed into the city limits of Carthage, supposedly for speeding. It seemed they were at the city line waiting for me. I had three of the local teenagers in the back seat. After searching the car, they ordered me to follow them to the sheriff's office. They proceeded to drive up and down streets while various cars and vigilante trucks joined the "parade." When we reached the sheriff's office it was dark. They told me to wait while they went for the sheriff. Meanwhile, the men who had followed surrounded my car, threatening and harassing us and pounding on the windows. In the car we kept our eyes on one another and quietly sang freedom songs together. The police finally returned with the sheriff (he was burly and wearing bib overalls!) and called us to come inside. On his desk were copies of articles I had written and articles about me in my hometown newspaper in Iowa. He read me an anonymous letter from a writer who expressed his disgust and hoped that the sheriff would "take care" of me for him. The sheriff tried to bait me with name-calling and insinuating that my motivation for living among "niggers" was sexual in nature. Getting no reaction, he fined me and sent us on our way. When we stepped out the door, the vigilantes were still outside waiting. It was a repeat of the fate of the three missing civil rights workers whose bodies had still not been found. I insisted that the police escort us back to Harmony, realizing that this was also risky. However, they did so, until we crossed over the city limit and the few cars following turned around as I sped into the safety of the community. This had obviously been a premeditated plan. An "Uncle Tom" in Harmony had alerted them, but I'll never know if there was a more dire fate waiting for me that fortunately was not fully followed through on.

There were other fear-provoking and violent incidents throughout the summer just in Harmony, as well as many other incidents documented throughout the state that summer. However, most of the time we in Harmony Community were able to go about our business, lucky to be in a fairly isolated rural community.

By the third week of August all the other vol-unteers in Harmony had left to return to their homes, schools, and jobs. I decided to stay on for another month or so, continuing to work on my projects and canvassing parents to register their first graders at the white school. Once cotton picking season started I spent a few days helping families pick cotton, though I was pitifully incompetent as a cotton picker. After school started, I focused on the library and literacy classes, and helping with homework, etc. I probably would have stayed on longer if I had felt more needed, and if I had not felt the wave of change surfacing in the civil rights movement. I had been recognizing a level of disillusionment, both on the part of some of the COFO leaders and among some of the volunteers, as the summer went on. There was a big discrepancy in educational levels between most volunteers and the "field secretaries" (mostly experienced civil rights leaders from Mississippi who were assigned to be in charge of the various Freedom Summer sites). This often resulted in many volunteers taking on more dominant roles in meetings and strategizing sessions, sometimes challenging decisions and undermining the leadership of field secretaries and even COFO staff, which naturally led to resentments and tensions. Also, it was a bitter disappointment throughout the Mississippi civil rights movement that the Mississippi Freedom Democratic Party was not seated at the national convention. In Harmony, a second great disappointment came when all the parents of first graders in Harmony backed out of sending their child to the white school. Only one first grader from Carthage followed through. Though the family suffered many resulting hardships, the little girl amazingly endured with no negative repercussions.

I felt a subtle shift among SNCC and CORE leaders from "black and white together" to "black power" and increasing cynicism about the philosophy of nonviolence. There was talk that Robert Moses was in conflict with the other leaders and might leave Mississippi. Although I let the COFO office in Jackson know I was staying on and would be willing to be helpful in whatever way they needed, they made no effort to communicate with me, nor did they ask me to work on any statewide activity. Even the field secretary for the Harmony project, who became engaged to Ms. Hudson's oldest daughter, showed little interest in organizing post-Freedom Summer civil rights activities in the community. Although the Hudson family was still involved on a statewide level in deciding the political direction after the failure of the Mississippi Freedom Democratic Party to get seated, I was not included in those meetings. Although all the families in the community continued to be very accepting and appreciative, I no longer felt I had a valuable role. I did not have the confidence in our relationship with the SNCC or CORE staff to confront their disregard for my willingness to stay involved. So I left in October, saying goodbye to so many who had inspired me and taught me so much. Before closing this pivotal chapter in my life, I made arrangements to bring four of the teenagers home with me for a week to Iowa, where we spoke at several meetings and on the radio to educate people and raise money for continued programs in Harmony Community.

My next move was to relocate to New York City and look for a social work job. Shortly after arriving I went to the CORE office in Harlem to volunteer. It was made very clear to me that they did not want white faces to be visible in their office. They suggested that I do research for them and send them my findings by mail. I completed one project but lost my motivation to continue. I came to accept that if I were to continue to fight for racial equality and social justice I would do so in my own way. I felt I heard the message: "This is our fight for freedom and equality, not your fight. We will fight the fight ourselves." I could accept that, though I disagreed. As Martin Luther King emphasized, no one is free until everyone is free. I certainly learned the validity of that on a very personal level. So it was my fight, too. However, I knew that I could continue to work against bigotry and social injustice in other ways.

Forty five years later, I stood before the Mississippi Freedom Summer Memorial at Western College at Miami University with many other former volunteers and veteran SNCC and CORE leaders and sang freedom songs, as we had done possibly in that exact spot a whole lifetime ago. Though there was only one other volunteer I knew personally, there was a natural camaraderie among everyone at the reunion, former COFO staff and volunteers alike, knowing we had joined together passionate in a common purpose and with a common set of beliefs. Maybe we had not turned the Mississippi white supremacy social system upside down in one summer, as we might have had grandiose hopes of doing in our youthful altruism, but together under the leadership of Robert Moses and other brave and brilliant leaders we had made an indelible mark on the history of the civil rights movement, as the memorial at Western College attests.

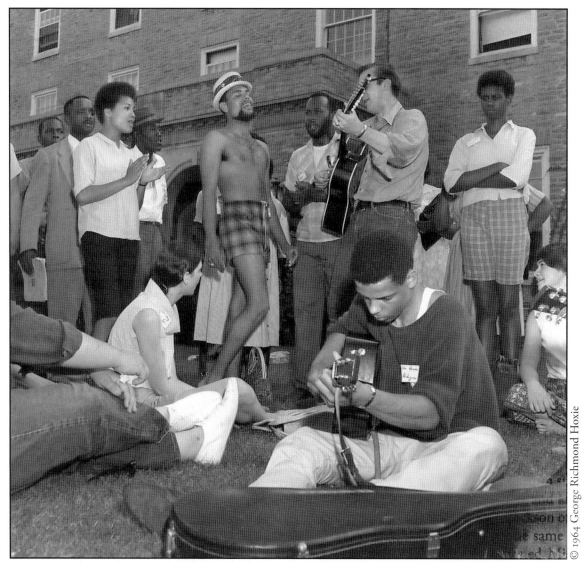

Freedom Summer volunteers and SNCC staff gathered singing on lawn in front of Clawson Hall.

Rick Momeyer
A VISIT TO OXFORD

The first time I visited Oxford was on June 20th, 1964. That was also the day that Michael Schwerner, a Field Secretary for the Congress of Racial Equality (CORE), left to return to Mississippi, where he and his wife had worked for CORE for more than a year. Schwerner returned with fellow Mississippian James Chaney, who had come to Oxford with Schwerner for the Mississippi Summer Project training being conducted largely by the staff of the Student Nonviolent Coordinating Committee (SNCC or "Snick"). Chaney and Schwerner drove back to Mississippi accompanied by Andrew Goodman, a student from Queens College in his hometown of New York City who as a Project volunteer had just completed a week's training. June 21st was the first day of training for the second contingent of volunteers gathering in Oxford. It was also the last day of life for James Chaney, Andrew Goodman, and Michael Schwerner. As many suspected and we all learned in the next few years, Michael Schwerner was targeted for elimination by the Ku Klux Klan. The KKK burned down a rural church in Neshoba County with the expectation that Mickey Schwerner—called by the Klan "goatee" or "Jewboy"—would drive out to investigate. And that was just what he did on that fateful Sunday, June 21st, 1964, taking both Chaney and Goodman with him. It greatly aided the KKK murder plot that Sheriff Lawrence Rainey and his deputy Cecil Price were part of the conspiracy. They detained the three civil rights workers until late in the evening so that the Klan could assemble their lynch mob. Then the three were released, run off the road, their car burned, taken to a site where an earthen dam was being constructed, savagely beaten, shot dead and buried.

Back in Oxford that Sunday evening, more than 300 volunteers, staff and trainers were gathering for the second week of training. Volunteers were to be sorted for their suitability to work in one of the three areas the Mississippi Summer Project had identified: teaching in "freedom schools," working on voter registration, doing community development work. But the real sorting was to screen out the too timid who might have survived the application process, and the unduly bold who supposed they were on a mission to "rescue" Negroes from oppression and that from their perch of white privilege they presumed to know how to do that. Most of all, the training was designed to impress upon volunteers the real dangers of proceeding to work in civil rights in the terrorist state of Mississippi in 1964 and to teach them how to protect themselves, their comrades, and the community they were to be part of, however briefly.

That training got very real very fast. By mid-morning on Monday, most of the SNCC staff knew that Chaney, Schwerner, and Goodman had "gone missing" sometime Sunday afternoon and that calls from the Neshoba County SNCC office to the Sheriff's office had not been informative. The veteran staff also knew that in 1964 civil rights workers did not just "go missing" one day and show up well and healthy the next; not in Mississippi, not anywhere in the deep south of the former Confederacy. That awareness was first communicated to the assembled volunteers on Monday morning, the first full day of training for the second group of volunteers, by Project Director Bob Moses. In his soft-spoken, powerfully charismatic manner, Moses told us what was known for certain of where our brothers had gone the day before, that they had not been heard from for nearly 24 hours, and that we should be very worried. The wife of Mickey Schwerner, Rita, also a CORE Field Secretary, reinforced this over the next two days by calmly, persistently, and powerfully communicating her concern to us before she herself rushed back to Mississippi.

The entire Mississippi Summer Project (MSP)—only later better known as Freedom Summer—had been conceived for the purpose of shining a spotlight on the most segregated and racially oppressive parts of the nation, Mississippi first and foremost. Many veteran civil rights workers had resisted the proposal to import upwards of 1,000 mostly white college students from the North and the West on the grounds that their presence would only ratchet up the violence of the segregationists and put Negro communities at much greater risk during and mostly after the volunteers had departed. But the more persuasive argument—the one that persuaded Bob Moses, the most important leader of the Project—was that true as this might be, the nation and its political establishments were never really going to pay attention to the horrors of segregation and its violent repression of human rights and human dignity as long as it was chiefly poor black people who bore the brunt of that violence. Not until the children of privilege—the sons and daughters of politicians, judges, bankers, teachers; the students at highly selective and themselves still largely racially segregated colleges and universities—not until these folks also suffered the brutal consequences of racism was the nation likely to do anything about it.

But no one anticipated, and certainly none of the COFO (Council of Federated Organizations) wanted, such extreme and immediate violence as the murders of three of our number at the very outset of the Project. This beginning, however, did focus the training of volunteers. Naiveté dissipated quickly, fear set in, courage was ramped up, trust was built between veteran SNCC staff and the volunteers, and the singing of the freedom songs, often led by the powerful presence and voice of Fannie Lou Hamer, took over. I suppose there were a few volunteers who left Oxford that week rather than proceed on to Mississippi—and a few more who were reluctantly hauled off by worried parents—but their numbers must have been very low. The seriousness, sense of purpose, and commitment to creating a more just social order all helped build a solidarity that was most evident in the singing of the freedom songs. Personally, I was aware of only one departure—that of an art professor from my college, Allegheny College, who had signed on to prepare students to teach in the Freedom Schools. I do not know of any students who left.

I had come to Oxford that week as SNCC staff to help do training in nonviolent resistance, to do workshops on the philosophy and practical applications of nonviolence in resisting injustice and promoting progressive social change. I had been privileged to learn what little I knew of such matters in some measure from workshops conducted by Reverend Jim Lawson when, two and a half years earlier, I was an exchange student for a semester at Fisk University in Nashville. While both were theology students in Boston in the early 50's, Jim Lawson had introduced Martin Luther King, Jr. to Gandhi's writings, and for several years prior to my meeting him in 1962, he had been preparing legions of Nashville students and citizens for nonviolent demonstrations.

Early on at Fisk I met many who had been deeply involved in "the Movement," as the struggle for human rights and dignity was known, heard their stories of sitting-in and going on freedom rides, and been utterly captivated by their excitement, courage, and commitment to justice. No one better demonstrated this commitment than John Lewis, newly enrolled at Fisk after transferring from the American Baptist Theological Seminary. It was John as much as anyone who drew me into the movement and enlightened and enriched my life immeasurably by doing so; and it was John, too, with whom I experienced, over the next several months, assaults with scalding water, bricks, fists and clubs; repeated jailings; a grand jury indictment on three counts; and the "freedom high" that comes with resisting oppression and injustice.

In the spring of 1964—well before my first visit to Oxford—I was preparing to graduate from Allegheny and John was Chair of the SNCC. I called him up to say that for the first summer since I started college I was free to work full-time for SNCC. John suggested that SNCC had ample staff and volunteers for the Mississippi Summer Project, but that Don Harris, Project Director for SNCC's work in southwest Georgia, could use help. Don himself, and three other SNCC workers, had been indicted the year before in Americus, Georgia, on the capital offense of "sedition and treason" for their opposition to segregation. Of course I agreed. Then John asked if I would first go to Oxford to help with the training of volunteers. And I agreed to this as well.

But in Oxford, I was largely superfluous. The far more experienced Field Secretaries were best able to conduct the training sessions on nonviolence, and my contribution was chiefly to role play a "victim" of assault and demonstrate how to fall to the ground, roll up, protect the back of one's head and genitals from kicks, and seek to protect one's brothers and sisters.

One of my more vivid memories of that week has to do with the daily mass marches we made from Western College for Women uptown to the Western Union Office on the square where a rusting water tower once stood. We were wiring our congressional representatives, the White House, the FBI—all to encourage a serious federal effort to investigate the disappearance of Schwerner, Chaney, and Goodman and to commit the federal government to protect civil rights workers. We must have crossed the Miami campus coming and going, but I have no recollection of Miami University in Oxford from this time. It was not until my second visit to Oxford, in the spring of 1969 for a job interview, that I realized that Miami, where I was interviewing, was in the same town as Western College for Women. It was the rusting water tower that made the connection!

When others headed off to Mississippi on June 27, I snagged a ride to SNCC headquarters in Atlanta and from there to Albany. After some time in Albany, Don Harris sent me and another Field Secretary, Herman Kitchens, to Moultrie, the Colquitt County seat. Herman worked on encouraging black citizens to take the considerable risk of going to the courthouse and attempting to register to vote. I worked on the Congressional campaign for the first black man to run for Congress from Georgia since reconstruction.

Herman and I lived on salaries of $10 a week and an additional $10 a week to rent a falling-down shack in one of Moultrie's two ghettos owned by an absentee white landlord and hordes of resident cockroaches. Among other activities, I distributed leaflets urging a vote for C.B. King in the upcoming Democratic Party primary, the winner of which would, in those days, be the next Congressional representative for southwest Georgia. In part this involved leafleting white neighborhoods and cars downtown, which, after all, is where those allowed to vote could be found. Such activities did not endear me to those residents, but the generosity and support of the black community was sustaining. Herman and I regularly, through the black community, were alerted to overheard threats from whites to bomb the house of that "nigger and his nigger-loving friend." Some nights we took them seriously and slept elsewhere. We did get assaulted in various ways, and except for being shot at, these did not amount to much. C.B. did not win nor land in a run-off, and in September I left Georgia to begin graduate studies at the University of Chicago.

My second visit to Oxford in 1969 for a job interview resulted in an offer to teach philosophy at Miami University. This led to a third "visit" to Oxford late in August, a visit that is going on 44 years.

One of the fringe benefits of living in Oxford was the opportunity to meet and become friends with Arthur Miller. Arthur was the longtime head of Oxford's NAACP, and a veteran of decades of struggle in the Movement. Not incidentally, he was also a very warm, smart, wise human being. One of the projects he took up on behalf of the NAACP about 1980 and thereafter was to persuade Miami University to own and to honor the civil rights history and legacy that it inherited when it acquired Western College in 1973. Even after raising about $25,000 to fund a memorial to Freedom Summer, the campaign got little notice from administrators at Miami. But when James Garland came to Miami as President, that changed, and soon the amphitheater that is the Freedom Summer Memorial today was authorized and designed. It is one of the ongoing ironies of that superb memorial that it was done in a hierarchical and centralized way to honor a grassroots movement by ordinary people to change the way things were conventionally done. However willing Miami's administrative leadership was to honor the history it had acquired along with the Western College, it was not prepared to engage in a process that the Movement created and nurtured, a process of grass roots organizing and democratic participation. Arthur and I and a group of Architecture students in a design studio did manage, however, to be heard to the extent that the inscriptions on the back of the limestone benches mark significant events of Freedom Summer 1964.

We are all visitors on this planet, in this life, wherever we go, and however long we stay. For me it has been a wonderful adventure to visit and revisit and stay a good while in Oxford, Ohio. I am grateful to the university that made possible a more than satisfying career as a teacher and scholar, but even more, proud of the university that celebrates its significant historical contribution to the struggle for human rights and human dignity in this land we all visit. The use of this lovely memorial to educate succeeding generations of students about the civil rights struggles that have shaped them, the university, and the country itself is highly commendable. Arthur Miller lived long enough to see this come about, and it is fitting that we should remember him for his lifelong commitment to the struggle for justice as we remember others who joined in that ongoing struggle.

Volunteers singing freedom songs on the lawn in front of Clawson Hall.

Phyllis Hoyt
FREEDOM SUMMER CONFERENCE AND REUNION SPEECH

The late Phyllis Hoyt was Dean of Students at Western College for Women when the Mississippi Summer Project training occurred in 1964. This is the address she delivered at the welcome dinner of the Freedom Summer Conference and Reunion hosted by Miami University on Friday, October 9, 2009, at Holy Trinity Episcopal Church in Oxford, Ohio.

It is my privilege to welcome you back to the Western campus. It is also a great joy for me. Students were my life, and I was here all the time you were. I stood by the bus that summer night and watched you go to Mississippi. The emotions of that moment are still vivid for me, and the pleasure of seeing you again is overwhelming. You are a different-looking group from those who arrived in the summer of '64. What is more significant: you are different individuals in many more important ways than you were 45 years ago, although your courage and convictions may be stronger. I am sure that the few days and your time together will reinforce those differences positively for each of you as you recall your own emotions and what happened to you during your time in the South.

My invitation asked me to share a few thoughts, and I am pleased to do so. As a bit of background that you may not have known at the time, Western College for Women (as it was called then) was a private, non-denominational liberal arts four-year college for women. It stated in its catalogue that it was a Christian college. The faculty, students, and alumnae had spent many hours debating and jok-

ing about what it meant in our daily lives. Then one day the president of Western had a telephone call from a friend of his who said that a group called SNCC was looking for a place to hold training for volunteers to go to Mississippi to register people to vote. He knew that we had held summer conferences on campus. The Western president called his senior officers together with a representative from the National Council of Churches, and they told us what they knew, which was very little, and asked us what we thought about the use of our campus for such a program. Someone said. "It is stated in the catalogue that we are a Christian college. Let's do it." It was unanimous.

I wrote an article for the Western students and alumnae in defense of the training and the mission and told of your great courage. The National Council of Churches circulated that article and, as a result, I had many letters. Most of those addressed to me were supportive. The hateful ones were destroyed by a clerk. Although I did not go to Mississippi I felt a deep involvement in all that was being said and felt by those around me.

My office was on the main corridor of Peabody Hall. I could hear bits of the lectures, and for some I moved closer to hear fully. Then I watched in wonderment as you took off your earrings, your sandals, your belts, cut your hair, changed into tighter clothing, attacked each other and assumed the fetal position as you fell. I saw you as you walked on campus alone or with a friend or two, heads bowed pondering the persistent question: Shall I go? Shall I stay? What will happen to me if I go? What will happen to me if I stay? I have never ceased to talk about that summer. For me witnessing your courage and your commitment was the experience of a lifetime. I saw belief become commitment and then action. Not just random action but concerted, well-designed action with a purpose. Your commitment became a model for most of the movements for social justice that followed. How many times in the last 45 years have you been asked, "Was it worth it? Did it accomplish anything?" You must have answered, "We were a force in the process of cultural change." That's powerful stuff.

The last night I joined hands with you in a circle outside of Clawson Hall singing "We Shall Overcome." By that time most of you knew what had happened to James Chaney, Andrew Goodman and Michael Schwerner. But you went. As I stood by the bus and watched each one of you board it I knew at that moment that our lives had changed forever. You are my heroes. Welcome back.

Volunteers gathered on lawn on Western campus in front of Clawson Hall singing freedom songs.

GWENDOLYN ZOHARAH SIMMONS
REFLECTIONS ON THE ORIENTATION AND MY PARTICIPATION IN THE 1964 MISSISSIPPI FREEDOM SUMMER PROJECT

My journey to Oxford, Ohio, for the Mississippi Freedom Summer Project began in Memphis, Tennessee, on August 9, 1944, in a three-room shotgun house on McComb Ave. At the time, four people lived in that house: my grandparents, Rhoda and Henry Douglas, and my parents, Juanita and Major Robinson. My parents would separate when I was three years old, after which I was largely raised by my grandmother, though my mother and father were actively involved. My grandmother, who had only a sixth grade education, was a born leader and organizer. I would later learn that I got much of my spunk, daring and initiative from her. She was a leader in our church and in our neighborhood. While she grew up as a poor sharecropper and knew directly about racism, she was no victim and taught me to stand up for my rights and to speak out against injustice. Though it was dangerous for a black woman or man to speak up during those times, she always did.

I spent a great amount of time in our church, The Gospel Temple Missionary Baptist Church, where I became secretary of the Sunday School and learned public speaking. I was president of the church's teen girls club, sang in the youth choir, and was intimately involved with all aspects of our church life from as early as I can remember until I graduated from high school and left for college. I was also very active in my school, Manassas High School, which I attended from the first through twelfth grades. I loved my all-black school and felt that the teachers and administrators loved me back. I was deeply engaged in the academic activities offered as well as many of the extracurricular opportunities. In my senior year, I was elected Ms. Leadership by my class and served as editor of our school paper and class president. I was also the president of my high school sorority of 20 young women, the Double Teners, who were considered the school's finest. When I left home to attend college in the fall of 1962, I went with a full four-year scholarship to Spelman College in Atlanta, one of the most prestigious of the Historically Black Colleges and Universities. I traveled with the well wishes of many of my teachers and my church family. My biological family could hardly contain themselves with the joy they felt knowing that I was off to college in pursuit of my bachelor's degree. I was the first person in our immediate family to attend college. My grandmother and mother who accompanied me warned me not to get involved in the civil rights movement, which was already in high gear there in Atlanta and other southern cities. The four black college students in Greensboro, North Carolina, who bravely sat in at a Woolworth's lunch counter on February 1, 1960, had launched the modern-day civil rights movement when they challenged the one-hundred-year- old practice across the south of refusing lunch counter services to blacks. Their sit-in caught fire immediately, jumping from Greensboro to Tallahassee, from Tallahassee to Atlanta, from Atlanta to Nashville, and on and on. In the first month 70,000 young people were engaged in this black crusade for justice and equality.[1]

While Memphis had been pretty tame in those early days of the movement, I was well aware of these burgeoning student outbreaks that were catching their local governments as well as parents and college administrators completely off guard. Once the local officials saw that these threats to their southern way of life were not going to go away, they began to respond to the student protestors with billy clubs and arrests. The white racists in these cities and towns responded with their own forms of vigilante "justice" by beating up the protestors, pouring scalding coffee on their heads and committing other sadistic acts. Images of violence were being captured on national television and broadcast all over the U.S. as well as in other countries. What an embarrassment it was to the nation as viewers from all over the world saw that longtime American citizens whose skin was of a darker hue were being beaten, tortured and jailed for ordering a cup of coffee in a five and dime store. Of course I was aware of these students and their actions, but I also was committed to attending college and graduating with a degree that would enable me to get a good-paying job, a new car, and hopefully a new brick house with more than one bathroom. My desire for freedom was sublimated initially to my urgent desire to leave the ranks of the poor and to join the elusive middle class.

I began my academic career at Spelman with my eye squarely on the graduation ball. Being in college was a dream come true, and I had no intentions of blowing my chances at the life I thought a college degree would bring me. I was assigned to an experimental history/English class with Professors Staughton Lynd and Esther Seaton, both northern white liberals. Little did I know that I would be introduced to an African American history and literature largely unknown to me. In the history segment of these classes, I learned about slave revolts led by fierce black men like Nat Turner, Denmark Vesey and Gabriel Prosser. I

---

1 Clayborne Carson, David J.Garrow, Gerald Gill, Vincent Harding, Darlene Clark Hine, editors, *The Eyes on the Prize Civil Rights Reader: Documents, Speeches, and Firsthand Accounts from the Black Freedom Struggle*, 1954–1990, New York: Penguin Books, 1991. 108.

also learned about fierce abolitionist women like Sojourner Truth and Harriet Tubman. My soul soared to the majestic words of Frederick Douglass, David Walker, and Ida B. Wells-Barnett, as well as to the writings of contemporary writers like W.E.B. Du Bois, James Baldwin, Richard Wright, Ralph Ellison and others who taught me about the long struggle of my forefathers and foremothers from the time we were forcefully brought to these shores. These classes certainly made the wheels in my head begin rolling, connecting the hundreds of years of black struggle with what was happening at that moment all over the South, even in Atlanta right outside the high Spelman gates. My resolve not to get involved in the movement was shaken.

Adding to the above was the fact that I had joined the West Hunter Street Baptist Church a few blocks from my campus, whose pastor was Rev. Ralph David Abernathy, second lieutenant to Dr. Martin Luther King, Jr. and founding member of the Southern Christian Leadership Council (SCLC). Every Sunday I heard sermons and lectures about the civil rights movement and the "righteousness" of our cause. We sang those movement anthems "Oh Freedom" and "We Shall Overcome" regularly. Dr. King visited and gave rousing sermons about the movement and how it was God's plan that we as a people would be free. These church experiences were also punching holes in my resistance to joining the movement.

The third factor that influenced me to get off the fence and leap onto this fast-moving freedom train was the fact that SNCC (Student Non-Violent Coordinating Committee) volunteers, most of them college-aged, trolled our campus regularly, extolling us to join this freedom movement. I was so impressed with these bib-overall-wearing revolutionaries that it was hard to turn them down when they urged us to come back to their headquarters, which was just two blocks away, and volunteer our time for our freedom. These calls really hit home since these were folks my age who had postponed their college education and their lives to work full-time in the freedom movement. In my heart of hearts, I knew it was past time to make the promise of democracy real for black people. I really knew that, even with a college education, I would still be a second-class citizen or worse in this "land of the free and home of the brave." I just had to figure out how I could join without losing my scholarship and disappointing my grandmother, neither of which I was able to do.

I began to volunteer in my free time at the SNCC office as often as I could. Just being there with these "jail-birds" for freedom was exhilarating. I knew that I wanted to be brave and strong like they were. Given Spelman's direct orders that we were not to become involved and their strict policies about our physical movements, I was literally breaking college rules each and every time I visited the SNCC Offices. I would lie on the required sign-out sheets, saying I was going to the library or the gym, or to visit another student in her dorm, when I was headed to the SNCC office or even more dangerously to a demonstration or a sit-in. Lying on a sign-out sheet about your destination was an expulsion offense, especially if it was repeated. I was doing so several days a week.

With the help of my roommate, Smithey Tuggle, and other classmates who worked heroically to cover for my absences, placing themselves in jeopardy in the process, somehow I made it through my first year of activism without being discovered by Spelman's administration. While I had been on several demonstrations and sit-ins at local public venues, I had been able to slip away without getting arrested. Yet I felt guilty as I watched my new SNCC friends get carted off in paddy wagons that shook with their songs of protest. It was a dangerous cat and mouse game I was playing with the police, Atlanta's "finest."

In my second year, I was elected by the Atlanta University student activists to serve as their representative to SNCC's Coordinating Committee. This was SNCC's executive body that oversaw its activities and decided which major projects SNCC would adopt for the coming months. One of the first big issues the coordinating committee addressed after I became a member was the proposed 1964 Mississippi Summer Project. The more I learned about the vision of the project, the

more excited I became and the more committed I became to it. Over my second year at Spelman, I became almost consumed with the Mississippi Summer Project. I had taken a second yearlong course with Dr. Lynd, one of the major persons working on the educational aspect of the project. His job was to develop curriculum for the proposed Freedom Schools, which were going to be an important part of Freedom Summer. I worked with him on this project as an academic assignment and became convinced that I wanted to work in the Freedom Schools project. The other two major components for Freedom Summer included registering as many blacks as possible to vote, either officially or in Mississippi Freedom Democratic Party registrations. The Mississippi Freedom Democratic Party was a racially integrated, truly democratic party that would contest the racist all-white Mississippi delegation for their seats at the 1964 Democratic Convention in Atlantic City, New Jersey.

Making it through my sophomore term without dropping out or being thrown out of college was a difficult task. I did get arrested two or three times during the term. I was caught lying on the sign-out sheets and faced the loss of my scholarship as well as expulsion. Somehow, none of these threatened possibilities were carried out, and I completed the semester. During that year I had signed up to be a Mississippi Summer volunteer. I planned not to inform my folks, who would certainly nip my plans in the bud if they got wind of them. Alas, the word did leak out about my plans to stay in Atlanta after the close of the semester, to stay with SNCC friends and travel with them to Oxford, Ohio, for the weeklong orientation that each volunteer was to have at Western College for Women. My grandmother, mother and uncle, having been advised by the dean of my plans, showed up unexpectedly on the last day of the semester and took me home against my will. After over a week of haggling with my grandmother and parents about going to Mississippi, I left without their permission on funds sent to me secretly by my SNCC comrades. When I told my folks I was leaving with or without their permission, they said that if I left I wasn't ever to come back. I left on that sour note for what I feared could be a rendezvous with death, as I too was deathly afraid to go to Mississippi. I had heard horror stories all of my life about the lynching, torture, and continued involuntary servitude that blacks in Mississippi endured. I could only image what those Mississippi racists would do to blacks (and whites) coming into their state to liberate their "nigras."

While I cried most of the way on the long bus ride between Memphis and Atlanta, I cheered up at the bus station in Atlanta when Dr. Lynd and his wife Alice met me and took me home with them. Once I arrived at SNCC headquarters I was buoyed up by the frenetic activity as everyone prepared for the looming orientation sessions and the actual proj-ect. I learned that close to a thousand students had been accepted for the project, the vast majority of them white northerners who knew nothing about the racism and violence toward blacks in the South. I was still scared to go but imagined that the fact that most of the Freedom Summer volunteers were white would make the federal government protect all of us. I did not believe that those Mississippi "peckerwoods" would kill other whites. I was to learn shortly how wrong I was on this count.

I caught a ride to the orientation with Dr. Lynd and our precious cargo of boxes of Freedom School Curriculums. James Foreman, the Executive Director of SNCC, put me on the SNCC payroll upon my arrival in Atlanta, as I was literally penniless. He was the one who sent me the bus fare for my sorrowful trip from Memphis to Atlanta. I started receiving my $10 a week paycheck soon after my arrival. I was informed that I would be staff at the orientation and would spend two weeks there helping out with whatever I would be assigned to do. I arrived with Dr. Lynd, who was also staffing the orientation, a few days before the first cohort of volunteers arrived, giving me a few days to acquaint myself with the beautiful campus, the college administrators who were taking a great risk to host this assembly, and the SNCC staff who would facilitate this historic gathering.

I remember the arrival of the other volunteers. They came with their backpacks, their sleeping bags, some with guitars or other instruments. Many of the men had long hair; some had beards. They had that hippie look. But most were clean-shaven guys and scrubbed-face young women who had come to right the wrongs that their parents and foreparents had let fester since Reconstruction. They were clear-eyed, dedicated and brave. They came with a certainty, it seemed, that they could make things right in Mississippi in one summer. As they would say to me: "Hey after all, this is still America!" All I could think of at the time was that they had no idea of what they would be facing. They had no idea of the entrenched feeling of white superiority, of the fear of blacks that fueled so much of the violence and rage. They had no idea! They were mostly Northerners from the best schools in this nation; they were from Harvard, Princeton, Stanford, Yale, Swarthmore, Oberlin, Antioch, Reed, the University of Virginia, Ohio State and on and on. I admired them and, in my heart, I thanked them for coming. But I told those I got to know: "Be afraid; be very afraid!"

I actually met James Chaney during that first week of orientation but not Goodman or Schwerner. Of course the world has come to know these three names, linked together forever as the three martyrs of the 1964 Mississippi Freedom Summer. But that first week was halcyon for the most part. The three hundred plus students went to lectures on the history of the South, especially its racist heritage, as well as about our tasks for the summer. We

had cookouts, impromptu concerts, and picnics, and we began to get to know each other. The main trainers included Jim Foreman, Robert (Bob) Moses (the Mississippi Project director who proposed the Mississippi Summer Project idea), Vincent Harding, Miss Annie Devine, Eunita Blackwell, Fannie Lou Hamer, Ruby Doris Robinson, Stokely Carmichael and many others whose names have dimmed in my memory over time. It was an exhilarating time. I was so glad that I had dared to come and be a part of this momentous event.

The first group departed and the second group arrived. Here I thought we would have a repeat of the previous week and then we all would set off for Mississippi—something that I still personally feared. Early in that first week, there was a break in the schedule and a special plenary session was convened. After we had all assembled in the auditorium, raucous as ever, we were urged to quiet down. As best I can remember, those on the stage included Bob Moses, James Foreman, and Vincent Harding. We were told that something terrible had already happened in Mississippi: three of our number, Chaney, Goodman, and Schwerner, had disappeared in Neshoba County a few days earlier and had not been seen or heard from since. We were told that Chaney was a native and knew the rules of making contact with the Jackson office or the Atlanta Office, if he could. The same was true for Schwerner, who was a seasoned Mississippi organizer who would have done the same.

We were told that the fact that they had not made contact and were no longer in the jail, or any other in the state, meant that they were most likely dead, killed by the sheriff or by others and with the sheriff's knowledge.

That information landed with a thud. There was an uncanny stillness in the room as we all tried to absorb the news. Three people—two white—dead already! We were in shock. We were told that we should decide if we still wanted to go; we could leave without recrimination if we wished. No one moved. We were told that those of us who stayed would receive intensive training in how to stay alive if captured and what to do in such emergencies. We were already being taught what to do, but now it was taught with a sense of urgency. Now we all were aware of what we were facing. Yes, it was still America! But it was Mississippi, America! It was, as Nina Simone wrote, "Mississippi Goddamn!"

Almost everyone stayed. I personally remember only one person leaving. I was assigned to Laurel, Mississippi, with two other African American colleagues, Lester McKinney and James (Jimmy) Garrett. We were told that Laurel had no real movement infrastructure in place and that it was too dangerous to send whites in at this time. My heart sank. The one thing I had held onto to allay my fears was the idea that the white volunteers would provide some protection for all of us, for the local people and the non-white volunteers. Of course the disappearance and probable murder of Goodman and Schwerner had already blown holes in that theory. If they were dead—and it certainly seemed as if they were—then it was clear that Mississippi racists would kill other white people if their "way of life" was threatened. While I knew this, I was still holding onto the idea that being on a project with whites might mitigate the danger in some way. That imaginary safety net was gone as three of us set out in McKinney's car for Laurel, Mississippi, headquarters for one of the largest Ku Klux Klan chapters in the nation. I was not reassured. I was scared to death and wondered if I could actually make the trip. My defense was sleep. I could not drive. Lester and Jimmy did the driving while I remained in the back seat sound asleep.

I did make it to Laurel in one piece and not only survived the summer but remained there for some 16 months keeping the Laurel Project alive well beyond the end of Freedom Summer. Lester, a seasoned SNCC organizer, had been to Laurel before and had a few contacts there. He was assigned to be the Project Director; I was to be the Freedom School Coordinator. We found housing in Laurel and moved there, setting up our office on the unenclosed back porch of Mrs. Carrie Clayton, one of the two women who took us into their homes initially; the other was Mrs. Euberta Spinks. Early into our time in Laurel, Lester disappeared without a trace. Needless to say, we were gripped by our worst fears! Frantic calls went to Jackson and

Atlanta; the Justice Department and FBI were called as were the movement's legal teams all across the state. Lester was found in jail there in Laurel. He had been picked up on an old warrant for his arrest stemming from an earlier altercation with the police. He had failed to tell anyone about this earlier altercation. A deal was struck for Lester to leave the county; he was not to return for five years or he would be sent to Parchman Penitentiary (the worst hellhole of a prison in the South) for a number of years. This left Jimmy and me, two greenhorns, to carry on with the project. I was given the Interim Project Director title, which was added to my Freedom School Coordinator duties. Jim Foreman assured me that this was just temporary until they could find a director for the project. He had not found one at the end of my 16-month stint as Interim Project Director.

The Laurel Summer Project was successful. Some 23 volunteers were assigned and placed. We ran a successful mock voter registration campaign, registering hundreds of black voters. We set up a vibrant chapter of the Mississippi Freedom Democratic Party and ran an oversubscribed Freedom School, which added a literacy component for adults and a Freedom Nursery School for preschoolers. When the summer ended and most of the volunteers returned home, three of us decided to stay longer and to continue the project: Marion Davidson and Linnel Barrett, white women from California, and myself. We stayed for a total of 16 months, joining with the locals' efforts to change the lives of all the people of Laurel, Mississippi, working on behalf of the principles of freedom, justice and democracy.

Three Mississippi Freedom Summer volunteers in conversation at Western College for Women.

MARK LEVY
A MONUMENTAL DISSENT

A set of multiple Queens College (Q.C.) connections brought my wife and me to Western College for Women in June of 1964, and kept us in Ohio for both the first and second weeks of orientation, prior to going to Mississippi.

Queens College, part of the City University system in New York (CUNY), is a public university and though not the often-cited "prestigious" Stanford, Harvard, or Yale, it too contributed greatly to the Mississippi '64 Summer Project.

I had been active on campus in "student rights" issues as 1962–63 QC student body president, and my wife, Betty Bollinger (deceased), had been the National Student Association QC chapter chair. We had been recruited to go south for the summer project in Boston by a SNCC staff person, Dottie (Miller) Zellner, also a former Queens College student and campus newspaper editor. SNCC worker Barbara (Jones) Omolade, also of Queens College, who did a lot of the campus recruiting of others at QC., did not make it to Ohio as she was assigned to SNCC's N.Y. and D.C. offices during the summer.

Early in the first week of orientation, we met Rita (Levant) and Mickey Schwerner, another young married couple who were CORE's staff in Meridian, Mississippi, and trainers in Oxford, Ohio.

Rita, too, was a recent Queens College graduate and Mickey's brother, Steve Schwerner, whom I had known at Antioch before transferring to QC, was doing post-graduate work on the faculty of Queens College's counseling department.

That first week in Ohio, Rita and Mickey asked Betty and me to be part of the Meridian Area project and to serve with them as teachers and coordinators of the Meridian Freedom School. They recruited another Queens College undergrad, Andy Goodman, to join the Meridian Area project. Betty and I were then assigned to stay in Ohio for the second week of orientation to meet and train with other volunteers who would serve as Meridian Freedom School teachers.

At the end of the first week, Mickey, James Chaney (another Meridian CORE staff person), and Andy went south to Meridian while Rita, Betty, and I stayed in Ohio for the second orientation week. Robert Masters, Nancy (Cooper) Samstein, Joe Leisner, and Mario Savio—also students who had been at Queens College—headed off to other project areas. History then abruptly—and sadly—intervened to change all of our lives. But orientation at Western College for Women and the Mississippi summer project continued in amazing and powerful ways.

While my life, from Freedom Summer forward, suggests the ways and extent to which I have been and am committed to civil rights and broader social justice issues, and while I appreciate the spirit that led Miami University to erect a memorial to Freedom Summer, I do have a point I wish to make about the way that the story of Freedom Summer too often is framed with the focus on the tragic and violent deaths of Andrew Goodman, James Chaney, and Mickey Schwerner. I can understand why they are so often selected to serve as symbols. These three men—two white, one black; two Jewish, one Catholic; two from out of state, one local Mississippian; two CORE staff, one summer volunteer—were brutally murdered while participating in an important struggle to make Mississippi and the United States more democratic and just. There are memorials to these committed and idealistic young men not only in Oxford, Ohio, but in other places as well—including my alma mater, Queens College. In speeches and books, the phrase "Goodman, Chaney, and Schwerner" is frequently used as a kind of shorthand to talk about Mississippi Summer 1964.

I would argue that there are a number of negative repercussions and questions that arise from so often memorializing those three victims and in using them as a method of telling the story of the Mississippi civil rights movement. I believe that we have more positive options for how to tell that story and pass the movement's ideals to coming generations.

First, as an organizer and teacher, I find myself wondering, when the three names are invoked, "What audiences and responses are being sought when these men and their murders are referred to?" Is the goal to elicit grief, guilt, anger, or inspiration? Is the tone mournful or heroic? Is the aim to instill fear or to encourage action? Is the desire to remember selected individuals or to build a mass social movement? What are the consequences when certain names are highlighted while others are overshadowed? Most importantly, how do today's young students, potential activists, and people of Mississippi sift through such contradictory messages?

When I remember my two weeks of orientation in June 1964 in Oxford, Ohio, what jumps into my mind is the profound respect I developed for the amazing skills and deep commitment of the organizers who recruited us and were trying to train us in such a short time. They had already found hundreds of brave, local people who offered their homes for us to live in and had secured places for us to teach or organize from. These organizers instructed us to be careful and respectful of conditions in the state and had created thoughtful protocols for communications, security, health, and legal eventualities. They taught us about trust and about racial and regional sensitivities. Importantly, they shared their vision of how voter registration, the Mississippi Freedom Democratic Party, and Freedom Schools in Mississippi could bring change to that state as well as to the whole of the country. I still marvel about how young most of them (and most of us) were.

Why not, then, find other ways—while not taking anything away from these often cited three men or their families—to put the emphasis on celebrating the value of involvement and activism, rather than highlighting its dangers? All the many layers of people who worked to make the Mississippi Summer Project happen—i.e., COFO field staff, local leaders, community activists, summer volunteers, Oxford orientation attendees, doctors, lawyers, ministers, actors, musicians, etc.—knew the long history of racial violence and intimidation in Mississippi. None of them or us—including Goodman, Chaney, and Schwerner—volunteered to be "martyrs." We, and they, wanted to be civil rights "workers"—part of the movement. The spirit of the struggle was "to keep on keepin' on!" To me, that's the value that should be celebrated.

Serious internal discussion preceded the decision of whether or not to undertake the 1964 "summer project." Both sides of the debate knew there were dangers either way to bringing national attention and large numbers of out-of-state volunteers to Mississippi, or to continuing the emphasis on local, grassroots organizing. It was a controversial decision. Today, nearly 50 years later, focusing on the deaths of Goodman, Chaney, and Schwerner reopens those tensions and that sadness for all in-

volved. Why not commemorate other aspects of the summer of 1964 that are more unifying and affirming, as well as educational and motivating for new generations?

References to martyrdom may sometimes be a useful rhetorical device and effective fundraising tool, especially for short-term purposes. I've learned over many years that this is usually not a good long-term organizing technique. The most productive volunteers to join organizations and movements (those who also remain active) feel strongly about issues that directly affect them; they feel they want to win and affirmatively believe that there is a reasonable chance to accomplish those changes; they trust the leaders and the leadership process; they have some fun and joy in what they are doing; and they have a sense there is not an excessive risk or danger to themselves. Invoking the names of Goodman, Chaney, and Schwerner, I've found, while an attention grabber, does not motivate people to become active; nor does it teach them about social justice.

"Empowerment" is not the feeling that comes from thinking about these deaths. Likely emotions are some combination of grief, sadness, fear, and even powerlessness. "They were brave but they got killed—so why should I get involved?" and "How could I ever live up to that standard?" are more common responses. "Maybe," a few say, "I'll donate money, but why should I get myself killed?"

No one—at least no one who would be an effective organizer—sanely volunteers to become a "victim" or invites others to become victims. Murders are sad and scary losses for our side.

How often, also, do we hear the civil rights narrative told in a historical way, as a story about heroic *individuals*? Everyone knows the examples and key phrases: "Rosa Parks sat down; Martin Luther King had a dream; Goodman, Chaney and Schwerner were killed—and now everything is all right." This kind of oversimplification makes many of us shudder every time we hear or see it. Telling the story in that way hides the fact that there was a mass movement that involved millions of ordinary people fighting for social changes. It also denies the complexity of the beliefs, lives, and contributions of Mrs. Parks and Reverend King, as well as of the mass movements they were involved in. At historical moments, individuals each decide to play roles as "upstanders" (as participants, or even as organizers) or "bystanders." It is important, moreover, to think not only about that kind of personal decision-making, but also to understand and appreciate the critical role that grassroots and large organizations and broad social movements play in changing the world.

I also feel that the repeated references to "Goodman, Chaney, and Schwerner" dishonor the work of many others. How does the incantation of their names get heard by the 1,000 volunteers who survived and worked all summer—and to a large degree continued those struggles for the rest of their lives—and by additional thousands nationally who actively supported the efforts in Mississippi? How does it get heard by the hundreds of SNCC, CORE, and NAACP activists as well as by the thousands of Mississippians who worked, sweated, and risked life, limb, homes, churches, and jobs all summer and who built the MFDP, fought against segregation, created and attended innovative Freedom Schools, and worked to exercise their voting rights? How do we teach about ordinary people like Mrs. Dessie Turner-Collins, who modestly but heroically offered her Meridian home to shelter my wife and me in 1964; or Roscoe Jones, who served as the seventeen-year-old elected student leader at the Freedom School; or the five young black girls who bravely entered the all-white local high school and the five who went to the white community college along with Roscoe Jones in the following years without the spotlight on Freedom Summer? Of course we should remember those who fell along the way, but more importantly we should remember and celebrate all the others who worked so hard and accomplished so much. Deeds—not deaths—are what's important about Freedom Summer '64. Deeds—not deaths—are "empowering."

We should also ask why mainly these three particular individuals have become—in the general public discourse—the symbol for the Mississippi Civil

Rights Movement and for the summer of 1964. Ella Baker's and Bernice Johnson Reagon's challenge is essential to remember: "We who believe in freedom cannot rest…until the killing of Black men, Black mothers' sons, is as important as the killing of White men, White mothers' sons." Why not celebrate Mrs. Fannie Lou Hamer? If any one individual deserves recognition and symbolized a range of estimable leadership attributes motivating many others, it is Mrs. Hamer. If we want the heroes and heroines of Mississippi remembered, why not create something that also honors women like Annie Devine, Victoria Gray Adams, and Unita Blackwell? If we need to remember those who were killed trying to exercise their rights, why not also memorialize Medgar Evers, Louis Allen, and Herbert Lee? The spirit and vision of Bob Moses and Ella Baker and the organizational talents of Jim Forman burned bright at Western College for Women that June of 1964—and moved many of us. Charlie Cobb was the initiator of the Freedom Schools, which we came to love and learn so much from. Why not have public reminders of all these contributions?

Yes, the murders of Goodman, Chaney, and Schwerner were outrageous, but equally so was the collusion of state and local government and law enforcement agencies with the KKK and White Citizens Council, the failures of the federal government, and the inability of the law and courts to effectively investigate and prosecute those (and similar) cases. That's the system of horror, injustice, and repression that was Mississippi. There are too many "unsolved" and "unresolved" cases still on the books and in our memories. Legally enforced segregation may have been ended, but what about the economic conditions, lack of jobs, overflowing prisons, poor-quality education, lack of access to quality health care, low income, and so forth that continue to exist in the state? What does citing the names of the victims of 1960s repression teach us about the issues that a whole social movement struggled to confront?

If I had to choose a monument or memorial style to cite as a model, I would point to the Franklin Delano Roosevelt Memorial in Washington, D.C. The memorial's emphasis is on the content of the quotations boldly displayed in it—stating the ideals, visions, and goals of the New Deal—rather than on celebration of the person.

I recently found some of my notes about the Freedom School teaching methodology and goals taken during the training sessions in Oxford in 1964. They were fascinating to read! The heart and spirit of the Freedom Schools had been mimeographed and sent us before we arrived and is reflected in these visionary, core Citizenship Curriculum questions:

» Why are we (students and teachers) in Freedom Schools?

» What is the freedom movement?

» What alternatives does the freedom movement offer us?

- » What does the majority culture have that we want?
- » What does the majority culture have that we do NOT want?
- » What do *we* have that we want to keep? [And do not want to keep?]
- » What do *neither* we nor the majority culture have that we would want in the future for *everyone*?

These framework questions, and the radical pedagogical ideas I encountered in the training in Oxford, did not only shape our work in the Freedom School that summer; they have stayed with me in my teaching and organizing since that time.

My dissent from the common practice of memorializing Goodman, Chaney, and Schwerner stems from my belief that there's much to be remembered, much still to be done, and more motivating ways to tell the story of the Movement and of that summer. More than citing any individuals or reciting the range of brutalities committed, I would urge that these Freedom School ideas be included among the inspirational markers to be passed along from our Oxford and Mississippi experiences:

- » Most important things to teach are that students must think, ask questions, and respect themselves.

- » Freedom School is *not* to educate students to move North and get jobs—*but* to form and motivate leadership.
- » We should not impose the ways we have been taught, but use ways we would have liked to have been taught. Also, Mississippi students will be coming expecting something different.
- » We will start building schools from the moment we get off the bus—and get into the homes and meet the families.
- » There are a lot of people in the community who want the Freedom Schools. Get them to help and to recruit.
- » You will often be the first white person the students know well. Must be honest—explain why there. Watch out for "Yes sir's." Students must question and talk back to teachers!
- » Learn "un-freedom" before you can teach "freedom." Learn from students how to survive in a totalitarian state.
- » A certain shared, basic emotion is "FEAR." It's a good starting point for a discussion.
- » Don't teach what's in your mind—but find out what is in students'.
- » Develop ongoing programs. Find and train people who can take over later.
- » Once a student learns to ask "*Why?*" the sys-

tem is starting to change.

» Must encounter people as people—not as "students" and "teachers."

» Get an understanding of the students' own schools.

» Compile history of the Negro in that county and of the Movement in that area.

» There is a dual responsibility of teachers to both prepare for school—and also make time to be close to students and to their activities.

» Not black and white—but "people" coming down South. No "insider" and "outsider." Eastland makes laws for all.

» If afraid of the unknown, should back out now. Can't predict. Can't play game by their rules.

» Everything going on in the community is a subject for discussion.

» Curriculum becomes a crutch for a teacher who runs out of words—the aim is to deal with students' desires.

» Examine words often used, like: "The system," "The man." "Mr. Charlie."

» Let teachers teach out of own strengths—both in content and in style.

» Medger was not killed just because he was the *leader of NAACP*. What he was *doing* was

the challenge.

» Evaluations by the students and discussions to see if *they* are getting what they want; teachers were invited to help them. One of the most important experiences this summer for the students will be their relationships with their teachers.

» Get to know the needs of the community: its general issues and the function of the Freedom School in relation to those issues. Learn the abilities of people to attend.

» Q: "Would you marry a Negro?" A: "Which one?" [Emphasis is that it is a *person*, a human being, that we are concerned about—***not** a stereotype.*]

» It's far easier for northern whites to work in the Negro community where we feel accepted than to step out of our shells and go where we are also needed.

» When the press does a story, the story is *NOT about you*—but about the community, the project, and the local people.

THE FREEDOM SUMMER MEMORIAL

Jacqueline Johnson
OVERVIEW OF THE FREEDOM SUMMER MEMORIAL

Dedicated on April 7, 2000, the Freedom Summer Memorial is a joint project of the Oxford Branch of the National Association for the Advancement of Colored People, the Friends of the Mississippi Summer Project, and Miami University. The memorial was commissioned to be a permanent reminder of the ideals of Freedom Summer and to recognize the contributions of all who participated in the Freedom Summer voter registration drive in Mississippi. It also honors the three slain civil rights workers, James Chaney, Andrew Goodman, and Michael Schwerner, who trained at Western College for Women in Oxford, Ohio and were subsequently brutally murdered in Mississippi. The story of their disappearance and deaths focused national and international media attention on Oxford and Western College.

Set beside Kumler Memorial Chapel on a hillside of the Western College campus, where many of the Freedom Summer workers lived and trained, the memorial is designed as an amphitheater with stone seating. It is used for classroom and informal group gatherings, and it also offers visitors a site for personal meditation and reflection. The memorial's stones feature 39 engraved panels providing a chronology of the events of Freedom Summer from 1964 to 1967 as reported by newspapers throughout the United States.

The Freedom Summer Memorial is a source of pride for citizens of Oxford and for alumni of Western College, which agreed to merge with Miami University in 1973. It calls through space and time to inspire the current generation to reflect upon issues essential to democracy and to remind future generations about the injustices of segregation and the sacrifices made by those who sought to end it.

As an archivist, I am familiar with the difficulties experienced by patrons seeking detailed information about the Mississippi Freedom Summer Memorial. In years past I have directed them to the Mississippi Freedom Summer Project 1964 Digital Collection (http://digital.lib.muohio.edu/fs/), until now the best source for information about the memorial. The site provides general information about the memorial's origins and dedication. *Finding Freedom: Memorializing the Voices of Freedom Summer* adds to the information about the memorial and the Freedom Summer Project available at the website, providing fresh perspectives on the contributions made by a small Ohio college and community to a watershed event in the American civil rights movement. It includes an account of the Freedom Summer Memorial's construction and photographs of each stone and its inscription. I hope that the book will serve the needs of those who seek information about Freedom Summer, the Freedom Summer Memorial, and the American civil rights movement.

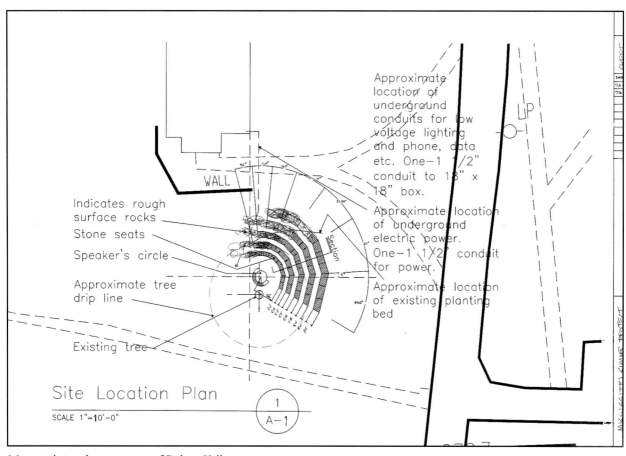

Approximate location of underground conduits for low voltage lighting and phone, data etc. One−1 1/2" conduit to 18" x 18" box.

Approximate location of underground electric power. One−1 1/2" conduit for power.

Approximate location of existing planting bed

WALL

Indicates rough surface rocks

Stone seats

Speaker's circle

Approximate tree drip line

Existing tree

Section

LIP

Site Location Plan

SCALE 1"=10'−0"

1
A−1

Memorial site plans courtesy of Robert Keller.

ROBERT KELLER
THE MEMORIAL DESIGN AND SITE SELECTION

When the opportunity arose to be involved with the Freedom Summer Memorial project, it was totally unanticipated and frankly not recognized for the opportunity that it was. I had been University Architect & Campus Planner for about ten years and, as such, had worked very closely with Associate Provost Joe Cox since the day I started in the position. Sometime in late 1998 near the conclusion of one of our regular facility planning meetings Joe said he had one more project he wanted to discuss with me. He and Art Miller, a longtime leader in the Oxford chapter of the NAACP, were in the process of raising funds to construct a memorial for the Freedom Summer events of 1964 and specifically for the three individuals who gave their lives for the cause that year: James Chaney, Andrew Goodman, and Michael Schwerner. My initial thought: OK, but what's that have to do with Miami? He patiently reminded me of the activities that had occurred on the Western Campus in support of the civil rights movement that year. Their goal was to memorialize those activities and the individuals involved. To seek support for the project they needed a site and a design for the memorial. I suggested that we could write a brief description of what was wanted and advertise a "request for qualifications" for a designer, which was the process we used for most projects. Joe had

other ideas. He was aware of my work in private practice prior to returning to Miami and knew that I had designed the Higgins Memorial on campus a few years earlier. Their funds would be limited, and he wanted whatever they could collect to go toward the cost of the memorial itself. He asked that we consider keeping the project "in-house" and suggested that I do the design.

Initially I resisted. We were very busy. The timing was not good. But Joe persisted, and he could be very persuasive. I don't think he was going to leave my office until he convinced me to do it. Reluctantly, I agreed to work on it *with him* and see what ideas could be generated. Shortly thereafter President Garland committed to supporting the project and appointed Joe Cox, Steve Snyder (Executive Assistant to the President and Secretary to the Board of Trustees), and me to work with Art Miller on the project.

The first time we met we discussed various ideas about the physical form the memorial might take. What shape might it have? What scale should it be? What kind of site would be best suited for it? Could the design be functional in some way? Joe and I had worked together on the Irvin Hall renovation project a few years earlier, during which was added the outdoor classroom in the courtyard as a result of a trip I had made to the University of North Carolina. Maybe the memorial could be designed also to act as an informal gathering place or to double as an outdoor classroom. But what should the memorial be? What should it say? What should it accomplish? I soon realized that to develop this concept any further I really needed to learn more about the events and the individuals that were to be memorialized.

Over the next two or three weeks many of my lunches were spent in the Western College Memorial Archives looking through old newspaper clippings and various articles from 1964 about the events of that summer. Sitting alone in that small room in the basement of Peabody Hall with boxes of old articles and black and white photos around me, I became absorbed in the summer of 1964. At times I completely forgot about what was going on outside of that room. I was immersed in events from that very different time…a period in our history that I hadn't thought much about recently. The headlines and the articles were very sobering. It was a stark reminder of where we had been, how much had changed, and how much change was still needed. How could the significance of these events and the ultimate sacrifice that these three individuals made be conveyed in a memorial? Images of the individuals and a plaque wouldn't be sufficient. Abstract forms or shapes with a few words wouldn't be sufficient either. Somehow more of the story needed to be told.

If we wanted the memorial to be a functional gathering place we needed a site that would be inviting, comfortable, and accessible. A sloping site would be nice, especially if it was generally oriented toward the south to take advantage of the early spring and late fall sun but also providing shade in the heat of the summer. If we wanted the casual passer-by to unexpectedly discover the memorial, it would need to be visible, convenient, and near a pathway. It was preferable that it be in relatively close proximity to where the training had taken place. After walking the area on two separate occasions, I thought I had found a site that met all of the criteria desired. Joe and Steve agreed. The combination of a maintained landscape next to a natural setting could be used to our advantage, and the adjacency to Kumler Memorial Chapel was an added bonus. It was close to Peabody Hall, parking was nearby, a major sidewalk connector was only a few steps away, and the views from the site were very appealing. We had a site!

The challenge now was to create a design that conveyed the significance of the events and sacrifices made in a way that could accommodate small to medium-sized groups of people formally or informally and responded to the existing conditions of the site. Could the design be something that was perceived in its entirety as it was approached, yet keep one's interest by revealing more detail as one got closer, as one moved around it and spent time there and revisited it?

Laying out the existing site's features and details on paper one quiet weekend morning prompted ideas about shape and form. The landscape changed from natural and unorganized on the west side to well-kept lawns, sidewalks, and a street to the east. The civil rights movement must have started out unorganized but gradually become more organized and structured as it evolved. Perhaps the form could begin somewhat randomly and become more organized as one moved around the site. More individuals and groups became involved in the movement over time. Might the form similarly change from a few objects to more objects and grow in mass and scale? Might it move from natural and unorganized to structured and organized? Very quickly, a form nearly created itself on the site plan drawing. From a single point on the west side of the site a series of rows of seats would grow and become more arranged as they curved around the sloping site to the east. This had potential. The following week I shared a very rough sketch with Joe. He encouraged me to develop it further. He thought we were going in the right direction. We had a form!

The newspaper articles I had read in the archives were still very much on my mind. I went back to reread some of the stories and dug deeper to find more articles to read. It was almost startling to be reminded of what had transpired. How could this memorial begin to do all of that justice? Many of the headlines alone were incredible when read in 1999, even without reading the text that went with them. Articles were scattered across the tabletop. I remember leaning back in the chair just scanning the story titles from newspapers from across the country in 1964. The headlines and article titles almost told the story by themselves. Maybe that was it. Maybe we could let the headlines tell the story as part of the design. Maybe we could combine these snippets of written text with a form that expressed the evolution, growth, and refinement of the civil rights movement that manifested itself that summer and in the years that followed. But, from all of his material which would be the right stories to use?

Joe Cox, Karen White (Assistant to the President for Event Planning), Holly Wissing (director of News and Public Information) and I had lunch at Mac & Joe's on a Friday afternoon and reviewed the dozens of articles I had copied for them. We discussed an idea: could we select a group of headlines that could be arranged in chronological order to tell at least part of the story as was intended by the original idea of the memorial? At the end of the lunch we came to the conclusion that we probably could with some additional assistance. We needed the concurrence and assistance of Art Miller along with the valuable insight of Rick Momeyer, a Miami faculty member who had been personally involved with the Freedom Summer activities on the Western Campus that summer. Soon we had the specific headlines selected and arranged chronologically and ready to be incorporated in the design.

The design evolved over the next few months, creating a form to symbolize characteristics of the civil rights movement and the efforts of the individuals that contributed to it. The form starts with a single rough stone in the west corner, as a way of expressing the idea that the movement was the result first of all of individual effort, owing a debt to each individual and to singular acts of conscience. More stones are then brought together, but they are not at first shaped; they do not fit together very closely and are only loosely organized. More and more stones are assembled as the memorial progresses across the slope; they become more refined and begin to work together more effectively, ultimately creating a well-organized, closely fit, and unified mass on the southeast edge.

Various means and locations for placement of the newspaper headings were considered. Perhaps they should be cut into the face of the seats so they could be viewed collectively from the front focal point of the memorial? But that would not be convenient for reading the individual lines and would be in opposition to one's orientation when seated. I thought it was important to create a convenient and comfortable means to sit and contemplate the lines. The final location of the text on the back side of the seating provided that opportunity.

Geometry is typically a strong influence when I consider designs, and this case was no exception. The geometry in the design includes the faceted lines of the shape, as these are determined by angles that increase in a specific ratio from the west to the east; the rows formed by stones that consistently increase in height and mass from the first to the last row; and so forth. I hoped that visitors might continue to discover new subtleties of the design over time.

The installation of the memorial was truly a group effort as well. The stonemasons who built the memorial were extremely helpful in the placement of the rough stones and with the transition from rough to smooth. They were led by a German immigrant named Heinz who patiently worked with me as we selected the rough stones from the pile, arranged and rearranged them, rotated and flipped them again and again, and hammered and chiseled at smooth stones to make them rougher in the transition areas, until they were finally organized as desired. Lynne Wagner, our graphic designer, carefully worked out the size of the text to fit into the design properly, and she worked with the engravers on site where the words were etched into the stone faces. Mark Cooper, the in-house project architect, worked out all of the foundation details and the placement of the lights into the underside of the stones. And our horticulturalist Bill Zehler led his crew to put the finishing touches of the landscaping around the memorial.

It took approximately 18 months to complete the project from the first meeting to completion of construction, culminating with a very well-attended dedication ceremony on April 7, 2000. I was fortunate to have been a part of the Freedom Summer Memorial and will forever be grateful to Joe for giving me the opportunity, and to all of those whose efforts and sacrifice inspired its creation.

Photos of memorial construction courtesy of Robert Keller.

THE STONES OF THE MEMORIAL

THE PANELS ON BACK OF THE SEATING REPRESENT A CHRONOLOGY OF EVENTS AS DE-
PICTED BY NEWSPAPERS AROUND THE COUNTRY, AND BY *FREEDOM SUMMER,* A BOOK
BY DOUG McADAM. NEW YORK: OXFORD UNIVERSITY PRESS, 1988.

THE MEMORIAL READS FROM THIS TOP BENCH >
AND SNAKES TO THE LOWEST LEVEL, ENDING IN THE SPEAKER'S CIRCLE.

Western College to Host Civil Rights School

The National Council of Churches' Commission on Religion
and Race will conduct a two-week instructional
program at Western College for Women, June 12–27.

THURSDAY, JUNE 4, 1964 - OXFORD PRESS

Civil Rights Demonstration Orientation Program
Being Held At Western College in Nearby Oxford
TUESDAY, JUNE 16, 1964 - JOURNAL AND DAILY NEWS - HAMILTON, OHIO

Mt. Zion Baptist Church burns to ground.

Fire starts after Negro mass meeting adjourns.
Three Negroes beaten by whites.
Church was freedom school site.

TUESDAY, JUNE 16, 1964 - PHILADELPHIA, MISSISSIPPI - *FREEDOM SUMMER*

Students Told: Watch Out for Klan
WEDNESDAY, JUNE 17, 1964 - CHICAGO NEWS, ILLINOIS

Students Warned On Southern Law

Rights Volunteers Cautioned
on Arrest in Mississippi.

FRIDAY, JUNE 19, 1964 - NEW YORK TIMES

Mississippi Rights Bus Leaves Ohio

Seventy-eight young civil rights workers left here late yesterday
on two buses bound for Mississippi, where they plan to
conduct a voter registration drive among Negroes.

SUNDAY, JUNE 21, 1964 - CINCINNATI (AP) - PINE BLUFF COMMERCIAL, ARKANSAS

Molotov cocktail explodes
in basement of Sweet Rest Church of Christ Holiness.

SUNDAY, JUNE 21, 1964 - BRANDON, MISSISSIPPI - *FREEDOM SUMMER*

Three civil rights workers missing after short trip to Philadelphia, Miss.
SUNDAY, JUNE 21, 1964 - MERIDIAN, MISSISSIPPI - *FREEDOM SUMMER*

Young Rights Trainees Scared, Dedicated

"If you realize that you may be killed and I may be killed,
the problem of being put in jail becomes very minute."

MONDAY, JUNE 22, 1964 - NATIONAL OBSERVER

Missing car found burned; no sign of
three workers. Car was on list circulated statewide
by Canton White Citizens Council.

TUESDAY, JUNE 23, 1964 - PHILADELPHIA, MISSISSIPPI - *FREEDOM SUMMER*

FBI Joins in Search in South for 3 Missing Rights Workers
TUESDAY, JUNE 23, 1964 - YONKERS HERALD STATESMAN, N.Y.

Knights of Pythias Hall firebombed.
Arson attempt on site of building used for voter rallies.
TUESDAY, JUNE 23, 1964 - MOSS POINT, MISSISSIPPI - *FREEDOM SUMMER*

LOOK, TIME reporters covering voter rally at Williams Chapel
chased out of town… next morning nine Negro homes
and cars hit by bottles thrown from similar car.

TUESDAY, JUNE 23, 1964 - RULEVILLE, MISSISSIPPI - *FREEDOM SUMMER*

Charred Hulk of Car Spurs Intense Search
WEDNESDAY, JUNE 24, 1964 - NEW HAVEN REGISTER, CONNECTICUT

Police, mayor tell summer volunteer he can't live in
Negro section of town and register voters.
WEDNESDAY, JUNE 24, 1964 - HOLLANDALE, MISSISSIPPI - *FREEDOM SUMMER*

Civil rights car hit by bullet.
WEDNESDAY, JUNE 24, 1964
CANTON, MISSISSIPPI - *FREEDOM SUMMER*

Hate literature from whites:
"Beware, good Negro citizens. When we come to get the agitators, stay away."
FRIDAY, JUNE 26, 1964 - HATTIESBURG, MISSISSIPPI - *FREEDOM SUMMER*

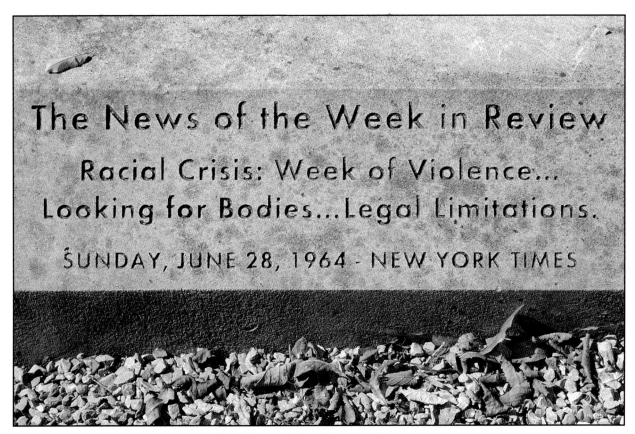

The News of the Week in Review

Racial Crisis: Week of Violence…
Looking for Bodies…Legal Limitations.

SUNDAY, JUNE 28, 1964 - NEW YORK TIMES

Freedom House call:
"You'd better not go to sleep or you won't get up."

FRIDAY, JUNE 26, 1964 - GREENWOOD, MISSISSIPPI - *FREEDOM SUMMER*

Oxford Blamed for Rights Meeting

The village of Oxford has received some criticism from the Deep South for the "Operation Mississippi" conference held the past two weeks on the campus of Western College for Women.

MONDAY, JUNE 29, 1964 - DAYTON NEWS, OHIO

Negro woman threatened for registering to vote.
TUESDAY, JUNE 30, 1964 - VICKSBURG, MISSISSIPPI - *FREEDOM SUMMER*

Pickup truck tries to run down SNCC worker and volunteer.
License plates hidden.

WEDNESDAY, JULY 1, 1964 - CLARKSDALE, MISSISSIPPI - *FREEDOM SUMMER*

Miss. Project Friends Seek Donation to Aid Work
A group of Oxford residents… who wish to further encourage this "Peace Corps type operation"
have formed a "Friends of the Mississippi Summer Project" Organization.

THURSDAY, JULY 2, 1964 - OXFORD PRESS

President Johnson Signs the Civil Rights Act of 1964

THURSDAY, JULY 2, 1964 - WASHINGTON, D.C.

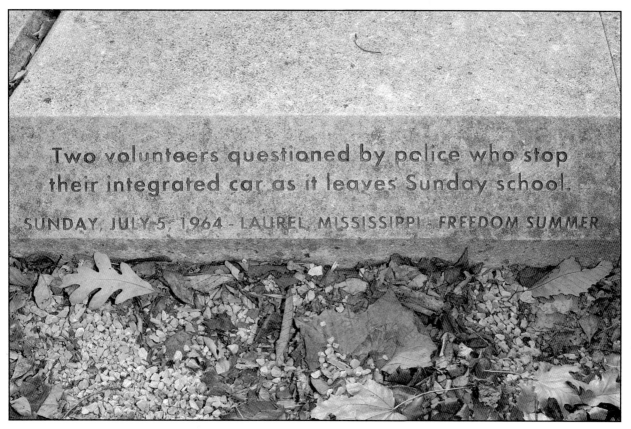

Two volunteers questioned by police who stop
their integrated car as it leaves Sunday school.

SUNDAY, JULY 5, 1964 - LAUREL, MISSISSIPPI - *FREEDOM SUMMER*

Negro woman shot twice at voter rally singing "We Shall Overcome."
Three Negroes arrested when they pursue car from which they believe shots were fired.

MONDAY, JULY 6, 1964 - MOSS POINT, MISSISSIPPI - *FREEDOM SUMMER*

Four young Negroes injured during
and after attempts to integrate lunch counter.
SATURDAY, JULY 11, 1964 - LAUREL, MISSISSIPPI - *FREEDOM SUMMER*

White Moderate Lives in Fear, Very Real Danger…
SUNDAY, JULY 12, 1964 - MINNEAPOLIS TRIBUNE, MINNESOTA

Bullets… Threats… Ostracism

"It is very difficult to sleep at night. It's so hot and then we are afraid of what might happen. The atmosphere is tense, oppressive. I'm not used to driving or walking around and being afraid I might not come back when I leave a place…"

SUNDAY, JULY 12, 1964 - BOSTON SUNDAY HERALD, MASSACHUSETTS

Freedom Day - 111 arrests, including 13 juveniles. Group includes
98 adults, of whom 9 were SNCC staff and 13 volunteers.

THURSDAY, JULY 16, 1964 - GREENWOOD, MISSISSIPPI - *FREEDOM SUMMER*

A Negro woman ordered off the bus and handled
roughly by driver when she sat down next to white man.
FRIDAY, JULY 24, 1964 - RULEVILLE, MISSISSIPPI - *FREEDOM SUMMER*

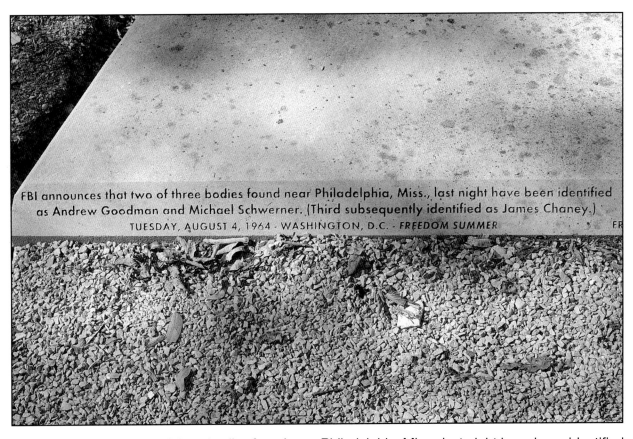

FBI announces that two of three bodies found near Philadelphia, Miss., last night have been identified
as Andrew Goodman and Michael Schwerner. (Third subsequently identified as James Chaney.)

TUESDAY, AUGUST 4, 1964 - WASHINGTON, D.C. - *FREEDOM SUMMER*

Over 200 persons gathered at four churches to take part in
memorial procession for slain civil rights worker James Chaney.

FRIDAY, AUGUST 7, 1964 - MERIDIAN, MISSISSIPPI - *FREEDOM SUMMER*

FBI arrests 21 in connection with murder of 3 civil rights workers in Mississippi.
FRIDAY, DECEMBER 4, 1964 - NEW YORK TIMES

Jury convicts seven of conspiracy to violate the civil rights of three volunteers.
SATURDAY, OCTOBER 20, 1967 - NEW YORK TIMES

This Freedom Summer '64 Memorial, a joint project of the Oxford NAACP, Friends of the Mississippi Summer Project and Miami University, was dedicated April 7, 2000. It honors the young volunteers involved in the historic voter registration drive of 1964 and symbolizes appreciation for the idealism of young people everywhere whose sacrifices have created a more just society.

James Chaney, 21, Andrew Goodman, 20, AND Michael Schwerner, 24,
trained at Western College for Women before heading south to register black voters as part of
the Mississippi Freedom Summer Project. They left Oxford June 20, 1964, and
disappeared the next day in Mississippi. Their bodies were found buried in an
earthen dam six weeks later.

ARTHUR F. MILLER — CLASS OF '49

1929 – 2007

THROUGH HIS TIMELESS EFFORTS AND GENTLE PERSUASION
"THE FREEDOM SUMMER 1964" MEMORIAL EXISTS

GLOSSARY

APWR—Americans for the Preservation of the White Race

COFO—Council of Federated Organizations

CORE—Congress of Racial Equality

FSMP—Friends of the Mississippi Summer Project

FMSP—Friends of the Mississippi Subsistence Project

FMFP—Friends of the Mississippi Freedom Project

KKK—Ku Klux Klan

NAACP—National Association for the Advancement of Colored People

MFDP—Mississippi Freedom Democratic Party

MP—Mississippi Project

MSP—Mississippi Summer Project

SCLC—Southern Christian Leadership Conference

SNCC—Student Nonviolent Coordinating Committee

UCW—United Church Women

WCC—White Citizens Council

CONTRIBUTORS

Chude Pam Allen is a member of the Bay Area Veterans of the Civil Rights Movement. Her poetry and memoir writings are on their website, www.crmvet.org, as well as in *Letters from Mississippi*, Elizabeth Sutherland Martinez, ed., and *Freedom Is a Constant Struggle*, Susie Erenrich, ed. She does public speaking and is featured in the award-winning film *Freedom on My Mind*. Ms. Allen was one of the earliest organizers of the women's liberation movement.

Ann Elizabeth Armstrong is Associate Professor of Theatre at Miami University of Ohio. She teaches directing, community-based theatre, and interdisciplinary studies. She is co-director of the "Finding Freedom Summer" project, a public humanities program on civil rights history. She has published on feminist pedagogy, community-based theatre, and intercultural theatre.

Keith A. Beauchamp is an award-winning independent filmmaker and activist who received widespread acclaim for his Emmy-nominated documentary "The Untold Story of Emmett Louis Till" and his extensive work in reopening the Emmett Till case. As founder of the Brooklyn-based film production company Till Freedom Come Productions, Beauchamp is currently the Executive Producer and host of Investigation Discovery's television series, "The Injustice Files." Mr. Beauchamp also assists the FBI with their civil rights Cold Case Initiative, solving murders that took place during the civil rights era.

Carole Gross Colca grew up in Davenport, Iowa. After graduating from the University of Iowa in 1964, she volunteered for Mississippi Freedom Summer Project. From Mississippi, she moved to New York City, where she worked as a social services caseworker. There she met her husband, Louis. They have three children and eight grandchildren. They were also foster parents for twenty years for older hard-to-place youth. After obtaining an MSW degree, Carole worked for twenty-five years in child welfare in Buffalo, N.Y. Now retired, she teaches social work part-time at Buffalo State College.

Rita Dove is a former U.S. Poet Laureate (1993–1995) and recipient of the 1987 Pulitzer Prize in poetry. She is the author of nine poetry collections, most recently *Sonata Mulattica* (2009) and *American Smooth* (2004), as well as a collection of short stories, a novel, and a play. She is sole editor of *The Penguin Anthology of Twentieth-Century American Poetry* (2011). She has received the Fulbright Lifetime Achievement Medal, the Premio Capri (the international prize of the Italian "island of poetry"), the National Humanities Medal in 1996 from President Clinton, and the National Medal of Arts from President Obama in February 2012. She is Commonwealth Professor of English at the University of Virginia.

PHYLLIS HOYT was born in West Somerville, Massachusetts; her family relocated to Wellesley, Massachusetts where she graduated from Wellesley High School in 1935. In 1939, she graduated from Russell Sage College in Troy, New York, with an A.B. degree in History; she received her Master's degree in 1940 from Tufts University. Phyllis's life was dedicated to her profession as an educator. She began her career at Lasell Junior College in Auburndale, Massachusetts, as an instructor, and served as Dean from 1940 to 1946. She was Dean of Students of Western College for Women in Oxford, Ohio, from 1946 to 1974. From there she worked at Russell Sage as Vice President of Student Affairs until her retirement in 1991. She retired to Londonderry, New Hampshire, and then to Peterborough, New Hampshire until her death in 2011.

JACQUELINE JOHNSON is the Archivist of the Western College Memorial Archives. She earned her Master of Library Science degree from the University of South Carolina and her Bachelor of Arts degree in English from Limestone College. She serves as chairperson of the national Mississippi Freedom Summer Conference that will be held on the campus of Miami University, in Oxford, Ohio, in 2014. Her research focuses on civil rights and the Mississippi Freedom Summer training and history of Western College. Western College Memorial Archives: http://westernarchives.lib.muohio.edu/index.php

ROBERT KELLER served as the University Architect & Campus Planner at Miami University from 1989 to 2012. He directed of the Division of Planning, Architecture & Engineering, overseeing long-range capital planning and major construction. In 2010 Mr. Keller was appointed Associate Vice President for Facilities Planning & Operations. He received his degree in architecture from Miami University in 1973.

MARK LEVY, born and raised in New York, worked at two careers. First, he taught social studies in a Harlem junior high and third world studies and community organizing at Queens College/CUNY. Next he moved to the labor movement as an organizer and administrator for the United Electrical, Radio and Machine Workers of America (UE) and the Service Employees International Union (SEIU) in the electrical manufacturing and healthcare industries. After retiring, he initiated the Queens College Civil Rights Archive, and he now assists with the Meridian, Mississippi, civil rights preservation and educational project.

RICK MOMEYER began teaching philosophy at Miami in 1969, five years after he had first come to Oxford as a Field Secretary for SNCC to help do training for the Mississippi Summer Project. In philosophy he has specialized in bioethics. After 43 years of such endeavors, he is almost ready to retire. Almost.

GWENDOLYN ZOHARAH SIMMONS, PH.D., is a Senior Lecturer in African American and Religious Studies at the University of Florida in Gainesville. She obtained her BA from Antioch University and her M.A. and Ph.D. from Temple University. She volunteered as field secretary for SNCC during the 1964 Mississippi Summer Project. After her stint with SNCC, Simmons worked with the National Council of Negro Women, and later with the American Friends Service Committee on a range of peace and social justice issues.

JANE CARLTON STRIPPEL moved from Corvallis, Oregon, to Oxford in 1958 with her late husband, Bob, and children Jeff and Molly. A Cleveland native, she graduated from Bowling Green State University, received her Master's degree from the Hartford Seminary Foundation (Connecticut), and did post-graduate studies at Miami University. Jane worked on the *Miamian* magazine staff, taught in the Talawanda School District, and was director of a community meditation center in Oxford. She especially enjoys visits with her grandsons, Rory and Jack, and renewal time in the North Carolina mountains.

ACKNOWLEDGEMENTS

Thanks to all those who made generous contributions to assist the Miami University Press in producing this book: Nicholas Money, Director of the Western College Program; Mary Jane Berman, Director of the Center for American and World Cultures; Timothy Melley, Director of the Miami Humanities Center; the Smith Charitable Trust; Oxford Community Foundation; and the family of Richard, Janet and Jayne Miller.

Thanks to Chude Allen, Carole Colca, Rita Dove, the late Phyllis Hoyt, Robert Keller, Mark Levy, Rick Momeyer, Gwendolyn Zoharah Simmons, and Jane Strippel for sharing their memories of a painful part of American history and of the construction of the memorial on the Western College campus.

Thanks to Judith A. Sessions, Dean and University Librarian; Robert Schmidt, University Archivist; and Elizabeth Brice, Assistant Dean for Technical Services and Special Collections for supporting this project with advice and collegiality.

Several colleagues have provided invaluable assistance with my research of Mississippi Freedom Summer since my arrival at Miami University. They include Ann Elizabeth Armstrong, Mary Jane Berman, Jerome Conley, Valerie Elliott, Curt Ellison, Dorothy Falke, Nishani Frazier, Elizabeth Johnson, Darlene Mahaney, John Millard, Jody Perkins, Jenny Presnell, Kwabena Sekyere, Mindy Stephens and Elias Tzoc.

I also wish to thank Mackenzie Becker Rice, Debbie Baker, Kaye Wolke, Cathy Cooper, Judy Waldron and all Western College alumnae for their continuing support of the Western College Memorial Archives and for keeping alive the memory of Western's involvement in the Mississippi Freedom Project. I thank Rita Dove, Keith Beauchamp and Spencer Crew for their generosity and words of inspiration.

Thanks to Keith Tuma and Dana Leonard of the Miami University Press for allowing me the opportunity to tell the story of the Mississippi Freedom Summer Memorial.

The memories and experiences represented in the writings express the thoughts and reactions of the moment.

The agreement between Western College and Miami University was signed in 1973. Western classes continued to be held until June 1974.

The photographs by George Hoxie reproduced in this book are used with the kind permission of Beth and Monty Hoxie for the estate of George Richmond Hoxie, and Valerie Elliott, Archivist, Smith Library of Regional History, Oxford, Ohio.

The text of the Mississippi Freedom Summer Memorial on the Western campus of Miami University offers a chronology of events depicted by newspapers around the country and by Doug McAdam's book *Freedom Summer* (New York: Oxford University Press, 1988, 253–57).

Miami University Libraries invites you to view the following online collections:

Mississippi Freedom Summer Project 1964 Digital Collection
http://digital.lib.muohio.edu/fs/

African Americans at Miami University Collection
http://digital.lib.muohio.edu.proxy.lib.muohio.edu/afamhist/

This book is dedicated to the memory of Arthur Miller, the Oxford Branch NAACP President Emeritus, one of the independent forerunners in the struggle for civil rights, and to all those who participated in the Freedom Summer Project.

"He has showed you, O man, what is good. And what does the Lord require of you? To act justly and to love mercy and to walk humbly with your God." —Micah 6:8

—Jacqueline Johnson